英漢 對照 **再譯菜根譚**

Vegetable Roots
With English Translation

金莉華 譯著
Translated by Chin Lee-hua

前言

金莉華

簡介

《菜根譚》的作者是明代的洪應明。他字自誠，號還初道人，在世時間，大約在明神宗萬曆年間（一五七三至一六二〇），生平不詳。除了《菜根譚》外，他還寫了《仙佛奇蹤》，記述佛老兩家的故事與思想，並有繪像考釋。

《菜根譚》敘述的是洪應明個人對人生的看法和處世態度，具有濃厚的儒、道、釋三家色彩。全書以隨筆的體裁呈現，言詞簡約，文字淺顯，而含意深遠。傳世的版本有兩種，一種是清乾隆三十三年（西元一七六八年）常州天寧寺校刻本，署名「洪應明著」，分上下兩卷，上卷標示修省、應酬、評議、閑適四個單元，下卷則為概論，上下兩卷共三百八十三條。吳家駒在《新譯菜根譚》的〈導讀〉中提到，該版本前有三山病夫通理寫的序。但清道光十三年翻刻的乾隆版，書名《重刻增訂菜根談》，書中的序則署名為三山通理達天。序中提到「重刻此書時，原書因年代久遠，遭蟲蛀腐朽得很厲害，原版又無處可尋，所以命工匠重新繕寫刻板付印。」另一種版本是明代高濂在其編輯的《雅尚齋遵生八箋》中的附錄本。這個版本署名「還初道人洪自誠著」，分前後集，書前有三峰主人于孔兼的〈題詞〉，全書共三百六十條。該版本流傳到日本後，由自署為加賀藩儒生的林瑜在文政五年（西元一八二二年）重新刊刻。這是《菜根譚》在日本最早的刻本。民國四年（西元一九一五年）奉化人孫鏘遊日時，購得由日人竹之恭編釋的此一版本回國，並加以校印問世，回流國內。該版本書前刊有「明還初道人洪自誠著，明覺迷居士汪乾初校，民國旅逖軒主孫鏘校印」等字樣，但刪除了三峰主人于孔兼的〈題詞〉。清同

治十一年（西元1872年），孫培之在一本道光六年（西元1826年）重刻乾隆版的菜根譚書後寫道：「余藏有小窗幽記四冊⋯⋯與此書相出入，未知二書熟後熟先。」如果《小窗幽記》四冊中的《菜根譚》與《雅尚齋遵生八箋》附錄本的《菜根譚》屬於同一版本的話，那麼乾隆與文政兩種版本的先後，早在同治年間就不可考了，但兩種版本歷年來都經過後人的增刪取捨則是不爭的共識。流通在台灣地區的《菜根譚》，大都以文政版為依據，但每一條的小標題則不知出於何人手筆，當必是近代人所為，因為孫鏘刻印的文政版《菜根譚》尚未標示小標題。這本中英對照《菜根譚》的中文部分，則是根據以下三個版本校勘而成：

一、《菜根譚詳解》。臺北：時代，民六十六年。

二、《菜根譚前後集》文政版。臺北：老古，民七十年。

三、《重刻增訂菜根談》乾隆版。《筆記小說大觀》三十九編。臺北：新興，民七十四年。

　　為什麼把書名取為《菜根譚》，作者沒有特別說明。三峰主人于孔兼在〈菜根譚題詞〉中認為「譚以菜根名，固自清苦歷練中來，亦自栽培灌溉裏得，其顛頓風波，備嘗險阻可想矣。洪子曰，「天勞我以形，吾逸吾心以補之，天阨我以遇，吾亨吾道以通之。其所自警自力者又可思矣。」道光年間會稽胡信樸在〈重刻菜根譚敘〉中闡釋菜根譚的含義說道：「古人云，吾輩須咬得菜根方能成得大事。此儒家語也。又云，性定草根香。此釋家語也。是編題曰菜根譚，其實能闡發乎二教之真詮，而具太羹之至味也。」于孔兼與胡信樸兩人的說明都有其道理，但洪應明將此書命名為《菜根譚》也許還有另一層意義。菜蔬是一般平民百姓日常的食物，物賤價廉。除了少數根莖類的菜蔬如蘿蔔、花生之類，菜根更是賤廉，稍有金錢地位的都不屑一顧。但尋常百姓卻捨不得將其扔棄，常把它們蒸煮入菜。筆者家鄉江蘇無錫，一般平民生日要吃連根的菠菜，平日綠葉菜蔬的根部，在稍加鹽滷後，加油蒸煮食用。因此洪應明認為，最平常、最純樸無華、最粗鄙的常是最好的，因為最接近本性，受到的人為渲染也最少。

從開始的第七條：「醲肥辛甘非真味，真味只是淡。神奇卓異非至人，至人只是常。」到將近結尾的三百五十一條：「山林之士清苦，而逸趣自饒，農野之人鄙略，而天真渾具，若一失身市井，儕伍儈駔，不若轉死溝壑，神骨猶清。」這種思想，一再重複出現，貫穿了全書。

翻譯

　　表達同一理念的方式與用詞並不是代代相同。例如"sibling"這個字，在十五世紀以前的含義是「有共同祖先的家族」。但到了十五世紀末，這個字就在英語語系中消失，直到二十世紀初期，又再度出現，它的含義則變更為「兄弟姐妹」。同一種語言因為時間的不同，會改變它的含義與使用的頻率，更何況兩種不同的語言，牽涉兩種不同的時空和文化。《菜根譚》寫成的年代大約在十六世紀，距離現在已經四百多年了。書裡的用詞遣字與現代的中文習慣用法已有出入，譯成現代英文就更需斟酌思量。這就成了譯者面對的第一個難題。洪應明心目中的讀者是當時的讀書人，當時的讀書人對儒、道、釋三家思想都不陌生，所以在文字上，他不需多加著墨，就可以將要表達的思想說得很清楚。如何使英語語系的讀者瞭解作者以言簡意賅方式表達的「另類」思想，而不產生誤解，是譯者必需面對的另一門大功課。《菜根譚》經歷了四百多年的時間，早期印刷術不發達，抄錄刻版的時候，錯誤遺漏在所難免，再加上歷代眾人的增刪，校勘也成為翻譯前一項重要而且費時費力的工作。這些在翻譯《菜根譚》時遭遇到的問題，譯者處理的方法及原則並非完美，只是提供一種或許可供參考的古書翻譯模式。現就上述的困難及其處理的原則說明如下：

1 中外古今文義有差距的詞句

　　中外古今文義有差距的詞句很多。以「君子」這個名詞為例。洪應明將《菜根譚》的讀者定位在「君子」。中國傳統最常被稱為君子的人有兩種。一種是在位的人，還有一種是才德出眾的人，一般指的都是男性。若將「君子」譯為"gentleman"好像很貼切，但是卻不合《菜根譚》全書的精

神。洪應明告訴我們，「善讀書者，要讀到手舞足蹈處，方不落筌蹄。」也就是讀書不可拘泥書中的文字，要讀書中的精神。他又說，「天地中萬物，人倫中萬情，世界中萬事，以俗眼觀，紛紛各異，以道眼觀，種種是常，何須分別，何須取捨。」《菜根譚》闡述的是一種人生最高的境界，以及達到這種境界的方法。書中論述的並無男女之分，只有賢愚之別。那麼「君子」二字在書中不能以「俗眼觀」。因為以「俗眼觀」，男女有別，女的不可以稱為「君子」，但如果以道眼觀，只要才德出眾，或身居要職，無論男女都是「君子」。

若將「君子」譯為"gentleman"那麼很明顯的將婦女排除在外了。古希臘人認為，一個能夠充分發展人性與才能的人，才是一個真正完整的人，也就是"a real person"。洪應明則認為，一個人若能回歸天賦本性，不做欲望的奴隸，就是一個天人合一真正的君子人。天賦的本性就是人性。兩者的用語雖然不同，含義卻是一樣的。因此翻譯「君子」二字時，就借用古希臘人的用語，稱一個天人合一的人為"a real person"。但「君子」二字在《菜根譚》中並不是永遠稱呼天人合一的人，所以遇到不同情況時，就分別譯為"an enlightened person"，"a real person"，"the virtuous"等等沒有性別區分的中性字詞。舉第四十二條及第九十五條為例。

42、超越天地之外　入於名利之中

彼富我仁，彼爵我義，君子固不為君相所牢籠。人定勝天，志一動氣，君子亦不受造化之陶鑄。

A real person is not confined to worldly wealth or power. His noble spirit goes above this universe.

Worldly position or wealth will not be able to slave a real person who values only kindness and justice. Neither will destiny be able to confine him, for his noble determination is powerful enough to remold his own destiny.

95、只畏偽君子　不怕真小人

君子而詐善，無異小人之肆惡。君子而改節，不及小人之自新。

Hypocrites are dreadful, but not the infamous.

There is no difference between a hypocrite and an infamous evil person. A repentant sinner is better than a saint who decides to sell his soul to the devil.

2 雙關語

雙關語在翻譯的時候常常造成困擾。《菜根譚》談論的主要是較嚴肅人生哲學，而非機智幽默的文學作品，所以造成的困擾較少。但要尋找在中英兩種語言裡同義的雙關語仍然是一件不容易的事。例如第三十六條：「待小人，不難於嚴，而難於不惡。待君子，不難於恭，而難於有禮。」，「君子」和「小人」都有兩個解釋。「君子」可以指在位的人，也可以指才德出眾的人。「小人」可以指平民，也可以指沒有德智修養的人。因此這句話就有兩種可能的解釋。若將「小人」解釋為「平民」，「君子」則解釋為「在位的人」來呼應，整句的意思就是「對待平民老百姓嚴苛不難，不過分卻不容易。對待上位的人恭敬不難，得體卻不容易。」若將「小人」解釋為「沒有德智修養的人」，「君子」解釋為「才德出眾的人」來呼應，整句的意思就是「對待沒有德智修養的人嚴苛不難，態度好卻不容易。對待才德出眾的人恭敬不難，得體卻不容易。」兩種解釋似乎都合理。因此就必須在英文裡也找出兩個可以和「小人」與「君子」向呼應的雙義字。試譯第三十六條如下：

36、對小人不惡　對君子有禮

待小人，不難於嚴，而難於不惡。待君子，不難於恭，而難於有禮。

Be fair to the petty. Be respectful to the noble.

It is easy to impose harsh discipline on the petty, but difficult to be just and fair. It is easy to be humble and submissive towards the noble, but difficult to be polite and respectful with proper etiquette.

3 古今文義容易混淆的字句

因為時空的差距，許多詞句在使用的方式及頻率上古今不同，因此常造成文義的混淆，進而影響到翻譯。例如第一二九條提到「害人之心不可有，防人之心不可無，此戒疏於慮也。寧受人之欺，毋逆人之詐，此儆傷於察也。」上句「害人之心不可有，防人之心不可無，此戒疏於慮也。」的意思很明顯。下句「寧受人之欺，毋逆人之詐，此儆傷於察也。」中「逆詐」兩字與現今的用法有些出入。坊間許多版本將「寧受人之欺，毋逆人之詐」解釋為「情願接受他人的欺侮，也不要在事先看破了對方詐偽的動機而表示嚴加防範的樣子，否則不但有傷自己道德反而更遭對方忌恨。」根據《重編國語詞典》（臺北：商務印書館，民國七十年）就「逆詐」兩字的解釋是：「事情尚未分明而先懷疑別人有欺己之心如『不逆詐』《論語‧憲問》。」那麼「寧受人之欺，毋逆人之詐」的意思應該是：「寧願被他人欺騙，也不要在沒有確切的證據之前懷疑別人。」這和《菜根譚》一百六十二條信人者，人未必盡誠，己則獨誠矣。疑人者，人未必皆詐，己則先詐矣。」可以相呼應。若以前者解釋「毋逆人之詐」，那麼「寧受人之欺」的出發點是懦弱，是害怕受到更大的傷害。若以後者解釋「毋逆人之詐」，那麼「寧受人之欺」的出發點是「誠」，是「不以君子之心度小人之腹」，是寧願自己受傷害也不願別人受傷害。前後兩者之間的差別猶如天壤。以《菜根譚》全書的精神看來，此句的解釋應該以後者較符合洪應明的原意，所以英譯該句如下：

129、戒疏於慮　儆傷於察
害人之心不可有，防人之心不可無，此戒疏於慮也。寧受人之欺，毋逆人之詐，此儆傷於察也。二語並存，精明而渾厚矣。

Both vigilance and trusting are important.

People should be vigilant. Intentions to hurt other people are forbidden, but precautions against potential malice are necessary. People should be trusting. Without good grounds to be suspicious of others is deviant and oversensitive. Those who know the importance of vigilance and trusting are wise and kind.

4 錯誤的字句

　　有些字句經過歷年的抄錄與翻刻已經失真了。校勘時，文政版與乾隆版若有出入，則採用文政版。舉第二一六條為例。坊間一般版本將第二句「不可因醜而生嗔」印為「不可因醉而生嗔」。一字之差，意思就完全不同了。道光十三年翻印的乾隆版《重刻增訂菜根談》中，此句為「不可因甘而過食」。一九一五年孫鏘刊印，老古文化事業公司於民國七十年翻印的文政版《菜根譚前後集》中，此句為「不可因醜而生嗔」。因為這本英譯本主要根據文政版，所以乾隆版和文政版有差異的時候，採後者。「醜」字現代中文常當「形貌陋劣」解，但在此當「羞恥」解。另外，第三句「不可乘快而多事」中「快」字當「順遂」解，而不當「快樂」解。因此英譯這個條目如下：

216、不輕諾，不生嗔，不多事，不倦怠
不可乘喜而輕諾，不可因醜而生嗔，不可乘快而多事，不可因倦而鮮終。

Don't give imprudent promises. Don't lose temper. Don't be elaborate. Don't be careless.

Don't give imprudent promises when happy. Don't use bad temper to cover a shame. Don't be elaborate when things go well. Don't be careless because of fatigue.

5 需要解釋的詞語

有些名詞必需經過解釋才能讓譯文讀者瞭解。這個時候採取兩種方法
處理。

（1）把解釋溶在行文裡

把名詞的解釋溶在行文裡可以減少閱讀時的躓頓。例如第七十九條的
標題是「心公不昧　六賊無蹤」。「六賊」是什麼？如果不解釋，讀者一
定不瞭解，因此嘗試把解釋溶在行文裡，英譯該條文如下：

79、心公不昧　六賊無蹤
耳目見聞為外賊，情欲意識為內賊，只是主人翁惺惺不昧，獨坐中
堂，賊便化為家人矣。

**If the master of the heart does not doze, the six thieves fail to cause
mischief.**

What we see and what we hear are the thieves from outside. Our undue
desires are the thieves from inside. Combined together they are six thieves
from six senses: color (eyes), sound (ears), smell (nose), taste (tongue),
sense of touch (body), and emotion (heart). These six thieves never give
up any chance to seduce their master. However, if the master is in constant
vigilance, these thieves can be reformed into family members who will
assist their master to do what is positive instead of what is negative.

（2）在文後注解

名詞必需解釋才能讓譯文讀者瞭解，但將解釋溶在行文裡又有困難
的時候，就用文後注解的方式說明。舉第六十三條為例，文中提到的歃
器」，現今已經失傳了，所以先音譯，再用文後註解的方式，將它介紹給
譯文讀者。

63、謙虛受益　滿盈招損

欹器*以滿覆，撲滿以空全，故君子寧居無不居有，寧處缺不處完。

Modesty gains; arrogance loses.

The container Qi^{**} overturns when it is full. The piggy bank will not be broken when empty. It is better for a real person to own little than to have plenty, to be improved than to be perfect.

6 不適用的舉例

四百多年前，人們的科學知識與今日有很大的差距。洪應明在《菜根譚》中用來闡述理念的例子，有些現今已經不再適用。舉例是為了幫助說清楚一個思想，一個理念。當例子無法達成任務時，不但不能替本文增色，反而是一個障礙，因此翻譯時遇到不再適用的例子，就越俎代庖稍作修改，以便闡明作者的本意。舉第二十四條為例，古人相信蟬是糞蟲變的，螢火蟲是腐爛的草化的，但現今已經證明與事實不符，因此將譯文稍加修改。

24、淨從穢生　明從闇出

糞蟲至穢，變為蟬而飲露於秋風，腐草無光，化為螢而翻采於夏月，因知潔常自汙出，明每從晦生也。

The dirty nurture the clean. Obscurity breeds glory.

The white lily is purely clean, but it grows in the dirty soil. The burning fire is gorgeously bright, but it comes from dark black coal. These are

---

* 欹器：中空時傾向一側，注水一半時則直立，大滿時傾覆。古代置於君王之側，作為諫戒之器。

** *Qi*: An object that leans when empty, overturns when brimming, and stands upright when only half filled. It used to be placed on the Chinese emperor's side to remind him to be humble.

the best examples to illustrate that the dirty often nurture the clean, and obscurity breeds glory.

7. 文意抽象難懂

洪應明在《菜根譚》裡用來表達儒、道、釋思想的文字，現代的中文讀者也常覺得抽象難懂，若直譯成英文，譯文讀者一定無法瞭解。要譯文讀者能夠瞭解，第一步譯者自己先要明白原文的含義，否則無法翻譯。這就牽涉到雙重翻譯。也就是先要把古文譯成白話文，再將白話文譯成英文。在翻譯的領域裡，雙重翻譯難度高，因為容易失真。《菜根譚》裡這類例子很多，舉第三四二條為例，英譯的部分其實不是直譯自古文，而是意譯自白話文。

> 342、就身了身　以物付物
> 就一身了一身者，方能以萬物付萬物。還天下於天下者，方能出世間於世間。

Fully understand your capacity. Share the universe with whatever is in it.

Only when a person fully understands his limitations and takes on only what is within his capacity, is he able to share the universe with whatever is in it. Only when a person stops taking the world as his personal belongings, is he able to live a divine and happy life on the earth.

8. 需要音譯時採漢語拼音

翻譯人名、地名等專有名詞的時候，根據翻譯的基本原則，應該音譯。中文音譯的系統很紛亂，常見的有威妥瑪、羅馬、注音符號第二式、耶魯、漢語等拼音系統。威妥瑪拼音系統在十九世紀時由兩位英國人Wade和Giles所創，已經行之有年。早期漢字音譯的時候都採用威妥瑪拼音。但是威妥瑪拼音的發音並不精確，所以在一九二〇年，林語堂和趙

元任另外創立羅馬拼音法。民國七十五年（一九八六年），教育部根據羅馬拼音加以修改，後頒布注音符號第二式，但兩種系統的接受度都不普遍。耶魯大學的漢學家在一九四〇年代發展了一套耶魯系統，用來教授中文，接受度也不高。中國大陸在一九五八年頒布漢語拼音系統。這個系統於一九七九年由聯合國採納使用，現在已經通行全球。因此在翻譯《菜根譚》的時候，遇到需要音譯的地方，都以漢語拼音系統音譯。舉第三一七條為例：

317、操持身心　收放自如
白氏云：「不如放身心，冥然任天造。」晁氏*云：「不如收身心，凝然歸寂定。」放者流為倡狂，收者入於枯寂。唯善操身心者，欄柄在手，收放自如。

Conduct life properly without going to extremes.
The Tang Dynasty poet Bai Juyi (772~846) said, "Let the heart go free. Let the heart follows its natural course." The famous Song Dynasty scholar Chao Buzhi (1053-1110) held different opinion by saying, "Discipline the heart to be serene." Those who let the heart go completely free are apt to become wild and impudent. Those who discipline the heart with strict rules easily become dry and dull. Only those who are masters of their desires can be free and serene at the proper moment.

結語

　　第一版的英譯《菜根譚》在民國六十八（一九七九）年完成，由成文出版社印行。這次重譯始於民國八十六年夏天（一九九七），因為教學繁忙，到如今才能定稿，也算是記錄個人的一種成長：一種對此書理念領悟

---

* 晁補之（1053-1110）：宋進士，工書畫，著有《雞肋集》等書。

的成長，一種將翻譯理論融進翻譯技巧的成長，一種對英國語文運用能力的成長。

2015.11.10臺北陽明山

【中文目次】

Contents

25. Suppress bad elements to bring out the good. Get rid of the undue desire to recover heart's original tranquility. • 053

26. Experience helps avoid folly. Enlightenment promises proper behavior. • 053

27. People in power should possess little interest in neither worldly fame nor wealth. People out of power should not neglect their duties to the country. • 054

28. Doing nothing wrong is praiseworthy. Providing no grounds for complaint is admirable. • 054

29. Don't work too hard. Don't reject worldly success completely. • 055

30. Dig the root of a failure. Observe the ending of a success. • 055

31. The rich should give. The wise should not show off. • 056

32. People usually don't see the danger of a high position until they reach a safe lower spot. People often appreciate law and order only after they have experienced the horror of violence. • 056

33. The person who can put down the undue desire is great and divine. • 057

34. Prejudice is harmful to a person's moral character. The ego is a big obstacle on the way to tao. • 057

35. Know how to step back and make way for others. • 058

36. Be fair to the petty. Be respectful to the noble. • 058

37. Preserve the fair and good spirit for the universe. Leave a clean name to the world. • 059

38. To defeat temptations from outside, defeat inside weakness first. To defeat irrational attacks from outside, be rational inside first. • 059

39. Weeding is necessary while growing plants. Choosing good friends is essential while educating the youth. • 060

40. Avoid the road of desire. Don't retreat from the road of virtue. • 060

41. Be neither wastefully lavish nor harshly stingy. • 061

42. A real person is not confined to worldly wealth or power. His noble spirit goes above this universe. • 061

43. Set the life goal a little bit higher. The golden rule of conduct in the world is to compromise. • 062

44. To develop moral character, one should disregard worldly success. To pursue profound knowledge, one should not be distracted by vanity. • 062

45. Good or evil depends on individual choice. • 063

46. Possess a heart made of stone or wood to develop moral character. Learn from the flying cloud or the running water to serve people. • 063

47. Kind people are warm and friendly. Vicious people are cold and malicious. • 064

48. If a person does not wish to suffer any visible humiliations, he should avoid committing any invisible wrongdoings. • 064

49. Suspicion invites calamities. Peace beckons blessings. • 065

50. Be flexible to conduct life in the world. Be adjustable to deal with different people. • 065

51. Forget our favors to others but not faults. Forget people's wrongdoings to us but never a kindness. • 066

52. A small favor without expecting any reward is worth much more than its actual value. A big favor with demand attached loses its significance. • 066

53. To stand in another person's shoes is a good way to make rational judgment. • 067

54. Wicked people use knowledge to justify their vice. • 067

55. Thrift helps promote integrity. Simplicity preserves the genuine happiness in life. • 068

56. The purpose of pursuing knowledge is to become a real person. A teacher should practice what he teaches. The fundamental duty of a government official is to take good care of common people. Only the achievement with solid moral basis will guarantee a long-lasting success. • 068

57. Read the book of conscience. Listen to the music from heart. • 069

58. Pleasure exists in misery. Sadness lurks in happiness. • 069

59. Ethical behavior enjoys the highest honor. Power-based reputation suffers the worst condemnation. • 070

60. Every person wishes to leave behind a good reputation after death. Every leopard wishes to leave behind a magnificent fur. • 070

61. Serious purposes and lively interests are equally important. • 071

62. True wisdom sounds foolish. Great skill looks clumsy. • 071

63. Modesty gains; arrogance loses. • 072

64. Fame and wealth bend one to be earthly. Arrogance and ego betray one's pettiness. • 072

65. Be fair and honest. Keep the thought unpolluted. • 073

66. Don't envy the powerful or wealthy. Don't worry about poverty. • 073

67. The covered evil is most dangerous. A publicized good diminishes its value. • 074

68. Destiny is powerless over the one who makes hay while the sun shines. • 074

69. The moderate are blessed. Extremes lead to disaster. • 075

70. Cheerfulness breeds good fortune. Evil intentions brew disasters. • 075

71. A real person should be careful of both his words and his behavior. • 076

72. Indifference is cold and barren. Geniality is warm and abundant. • 076

73. The road of righteousness is broad. The road of desire is narrow. • 077

74. Blessings obtained after numerous hardships last long. Knowledge gained after much deliberation is real. • 077

75. Empty the heart to make room for moral teachings. Stuff the heart with upright principles to ward off improper desires. • 078

76. Genuine kindness discriminates against none. True tolerance accepts differences. • 078

77. Tough times and hard work help build a strong and prosperous country. Comfortable life and jolly amusements ruin a person's life. • 079

78. The slightest touch of avarice leads a person to an eternal fall. • 079

79. If the master of the heart does not doze, the six thieves fail to cause mischief. • 080

80. Work hard on the present achievement to ensure a bright future. • 080

81. Cultivate the upright qualities of the universe. Follow the examples of real people of the present and the past. • 081

82. Keep neither image nor sound. • 081

83. A real person's behavior never goes to extremes. • 082

84. Redouble efforts to reach the goal during times of adversity. Lose neither confidence nor dignity. • 082

85. Prepare for the rain before it comes. There will be no danger when there is adequate preparation. • 083

86. To rein in the horse at the edge of a cliff is to save life from mortal danger. • 083

87. The best way to understand one's own heart is when serene without any undue desire. • 084

88. To be composed in turmoil . To stay joyful in hardship. • 084

89. Make sacrifices without hesitation. Perform good deeds without expecting a reward. • 085

90. Accumulate good deeds to increase chances for good fortune, suppress undue desires to ease physical and mental fatigue, and behave conscientiously to shun misfortune. • 085

91. God blesses those who don't pursue personal profit but condemns those who shun personal loss. • 086

92. The final ending is what counts in a person's life. The harvest is what matters in planting. • 086

93. Be diligent in doing what is good and kind. Be greedy for neither power nor wealth. • 087

94. It is difficult to build but easy to destroy. • 087

95. Hypocrites are dreadful, but not necessary the infamous. • 088

96. Spring wind thaws frozen earth. Geniality dissolves an icy atmosphere. • 088

97. Sincerity, generosity, and justice lead to a peaceful and happy world. • 089

98. Don't bend principles. Don't flaunt fine qualities. • 089

99. Don't be exultant in prosperity. Don't be depressed in adversity. • 090

100. When the wealthy and powerful abuse their privileges, they are digging their own graves. • 090

101. Even an unyielding rock can be moved by sincerity. • 091

102. An excellent piece of writing does not need special skills. The best character is without any fancy adornment. • 091

103. Distinguish reality from illusion. Take on important responsibilities to serve the world. • 092

104. Don't go to extremes. Moderation prevents misfortune and regrets. • 092

105. Forgiveness and trustiness are effective ways to cultivate a good character and keep troubles away. • 093

106. Behave with dignity. Possess no strong passions. • 093

107. Life is not eternal. Don't waste it. • 094

108. Remember neither favors nor enmity. Forget both hostility and kindness. • 094

109. Be careful when in the glory of success. • 095

110. Support public justice but not personal favors. Cultivate good character and accumulate good deeds. • 095

111. Don't offend against fair public opinion. Don't flatter the powerful. • 096

112. Integrity fears no bitter feelings. Moral excellence fears no slanders. • 096

113. Be composed in facing family conflicts. Be sincere about a friend's mistake. • 097

114. Be farsighted, but begin with the very fundamental. • 097

115. Strong passions evolve into hostility. Insignificant but timely assistance results in great joy. • 098

116. Hide ingenuity behind crudeness. Conceal purity in muddiness. • 098

117. The peak of prosperity foretells decline. The ultimate end of despair is hope. • 099

118. Novelty wears off soon. Austerity does not last long. • 099

119. Put down the butcher's knife to become buddha at once. • 100

120. Don't listen to only one side of the story nor be obstinate. Be neither self-conceited nor jealous of other people. • 100

121. Don't attack people's shortcomings. Don't be headstrong towards the stubborn. • 101

122. Be reserved towards the sneaky. Be quiet with the proud. • 101

123. Use the deafening sound to make the deaf hear. Use the blinding light to make the blind see. Act prudently as at the edge of a high cliff and as on the surface of the thin ice. • 102

1、弄權一時　淒涼萬古

棲守道德者，寂寞一時；依阿權勢者，淒涼萬古。達人觀物外之物，思身後之身，寧受一時之寂寞，毋取萬古之淒涼。

A moment of power exchanges for eternal loneliness.

For those who observe the moral principle, loneliness is only temporary, but for those who surrender to power and wealth, loneliness will be eternal. An enlightened person evaluates things beyond their material value, and plans for life beyond its temporal existence. He is willing to suffer loneliness temporarily, but not to be rejected eternally.

2、抱樸守拙　涉世之道

涉世淺，點染亦淺；歷事深，機械亦深。故君子與其練達，不若樸魯；與其曲謹，不若疏狂。

Simplicity and honesty are good ways to conduct life in this world.

Being innocent of worldly shrewdness is innocent of sophistication. Sophistication is not far from cunning. It is better to be simple and honest than to be shrewd and sophisticated.

3、心事宜明　才華須韞

君子之心事，似青天白日，不可使人不知；君子之才華，玉韞珠藏，不可使人易知。

Disclose intention, but conceal ability.

A real person's intention, which is like the bright sun in the blue sky, is void of any shadow of evil; therefore, there is no reason to conceal it. A real person's ability, which is like the precious stone or the valuable pearl, is easy to attract jealousy, so it should be carefully treasured instead of any unnecessary exposure.

4、出汙泥而不染　明機巧而不用

勢利紛華，不近者為潔，近之而不染者尤潔；智械機巧，不知者為高，知之而不用者為尤高。

Keep clean in the mud. Reject cunning maneuvers.

Chasing neither power nor wealth is clean. Possessing both power and wealth but without being contaminated by them is even cleaner. Knowing no cunning tricks is admirable. Knowing various cunning tricks but refusing to use them is even more admirable.

5、良藥苦口　忠言逆耳

耳中常聞逆耳之言，心中常有拂心之事，纔是進德修行的砥石。若言言樂耳，事事快心，便把此身埋在鴆毒中矣。

Effective medicine tastes bitter. Good advice sounds dreadful.

Harsh criticism and unpleasant experience often improve a person's moral character. Black calamity usually lurks in rosy good fortune.

6、和氣致祥　喜氣多瑞

疾風怒雨，禽鳥戚戚；霽日風光，草木欣欣。可見天地不可一日無和氣，人心不可一日無喜神。

Geniality leads to good fortune. Cheerfulness brings favorable results.

While biting wind and angry rain sadden the whole universe, warm sunshine and gentle breeze bring life to the earth. It exemplifies that geniality is essential to the universe, and cheerfulness is indispensable to human beings.

7、淡中知真味　常裡識英雄

醲肥辛甘非真味，真味只是淡；神奇卓異非至人，至人只是常。

True flavor is found in unseasoned food. Heroic and noble qualities are realized in common behavior.

Richly seasoned food has lost its genuine flavor. The true flavor of food is plain. Extraordinary talent or intelligence is not the quality of a noble character. The real quality of a noble character is simply ordinary and common.

8、閒時吃緊　忙裡悠閒

天地寂然不動，而氣機無息稍停；日月盡夜奔馳，而貞明萬古不易。故君子閒時要有吃緊的心思，忙處要有悠閒的趣味。

Don't slow down when unoccupied. Relax when heavily engaged.

Although people do not feel the movement of time, time never halts its steps. Although the day and night have never ceased chasing each other, they show little sign of hastiness. A real person will not waste his time when unoccupied, nor will he be in any rush when heavily engaged.

9、靜中觀心　真妄畢見

夜深人靜，獨坐觀心，始覺妄窮而真獨露，每於此中得大機趣；既覺真現而妄難逃，又於此中得大慚忸。

Look into your conscience quietly; the truth emerges.

Sitting alone in a quiet night to look into your conscience, you will find out the truth from the fiction. The result often pleases and shames you simultaneously.

10、得意須早回頭　拂心莫便放手

恩裡由來生害，故快意時須早回首；敗後或反成功，故拂心處莫便放手。

Quit while ahead. Stay while behind.

Glory is often the disaster in disguise. It is wise to put it down as soon as possible. Setbacks often herald success. It is advisable to hold on and face the challenge.

11、澹泊明志　肥甘喪節

藜口莧腸者，多冰清玉潔；袞衣玉食者，甘婢膝奴顏。蓋志以澹泊明，而節從肥甘喪也。

Simple life cultivates noble character. Extravagance erodes good principles in life.

One who can endure poverty usually possesses good character. Those who long for wealth and power, more often than not, have to bend to reach their goal. It is said that noble character comes from simple life, and extravagance erodes moral principles.

12、眼前放得寬大　死後恩澤悠久

面前的田地要放得寬，使人無不平之嘆；身後的恩澤要流得久，使人有不匱之思。

Be generous, and the good result will last long after death.

Be generous. Your kindness will not only be appreciated now but long felt and remembered even after death.

13、路要讓一步　味須減三分

路徑窄處，留一步與人行；滋味濃的，減三分讓人嚐。此是涉世一極樂法。

Make way for people to pass on a narrow road. Share with people what is nice and sweet.

Making way for people to pass on a narrow road and sharing with people what is nice and sweet promise a peaceful and happy life.

14、脫俗成名　超凡入聖

做人無甚高遠事業，擺脫得俗情，便入名流；為學無甚增益功夫，減除得物累，便超聖境。

Chasing not worldly power or wealth is outstanding. Cutting down worldly desires increases wisdom.

It is easy to be outstanding after stopping chasing worldly power or wealth. It is not difficult to be an enlightened person after cutting down worldly desires.

15、義俠交友　純心做人

交友須帶三分俠氣，做人要存一點素心。

Being helpful and unselfish are important to cultivate friendships. Sincerity is indispensable to be a real person.

Being willing to help and being unselfish are essential qualities in making friends. To be a real person, sincerity is indispensable.

16、德在人先　利在人後

寵利毋居人前，德業毋落人後，受享毋踰分外，修為毋減分中。

Be first to do what is ethical. Be last to collect rewards.

Don't compete for profits. Don't be slow in doing what is ethical. Don't accept what is more than deserved. Don't relax efforts on developing moral character.

17、退即是進　與即是得

處世讓一步為高，退步即進步的張本；待人寬一分是福，利人實利己的根基。

To retreat is to advance. To give is to gain.

To retreat is the supreme rule of conduct in this world, for it heralds advancement. The generous and kind are blessed, for those who give shall be given.

18、驕矜無功　懺悔滅罪

蓋世功勞，當不得一個矜字；彌天罪過，當不得一個悔字。

Pride ruins achievement. Repentance cleans sin.

No matter how great the achievement is, arrogance ruins the greatness. No matter how destructive the crime is, repentance purifies the sin.

19、完名讓人全身遠害　歸咎於己韜光養德

完名美節，不宜獨任，分些與人，可以遠害全身；辱行汙名，不宜全推，引些歸己，可以韜光養德。

Share credit with other people to keep evils away. Accept the blame to cultivate moral character.

Don't take all the credit for a success. To share credit with those who make the success possible to keep away complaints and vicious attacks. Don't deny all the blame for a failure. To take the blame with those who cause the failure to cultivate moral character.

20、天道忌盈　卦終未濟

事事留個有餘不盡的意思，便造物不能忌我，鬼神不能損我。若業必求滿，功必求盈者，不生內變，必召外憂。

The Creator of this universe prohibits good fortune to its fullness. Good fortune to its fullness leads to calamity.

Neither the Creator nor the Supernatural beings will be able to harm those who always share good fortune with others. Those who claim good fortune to its fullest extent will surely suffer damage from either inside or outside.

21、人能誠心和氣　勝於調息觀心

家庭有個真佛，日用有種真道，人能誠心和氣，愉色婉言，使父母兄弟間，形骸兩釋，意氣交流，勝於調息觀心萬倍矣。

Sincerity and geniality is better than meditation.

The final goal of meditation is to live harmoniously with oneself and with the universe. However, to have a divine guidance in the family, to live each day honestly, to be genial and sincere towards people, and to keep good relationships with family members are better ways to reach the goal.

22、動靜合宜　道之真體

好動者，雲電風燈；嗜寂者，死灰槁木；需定雲止水中，有鳶飛魚躍氣象，才是有道的心體。

Tao is to moderate the extremes. Its essence is balance.

An active person is like the lightning in the sky or the lamp in the storm. His action is bursting with energy but short-lived. A quiet person is similar to the cold ash after fire is gone or the dried wood after life has left. He is peaceful but lifeless. Neither is recommended. An enlightened person should take lessons from the reflections of the drifting clouds in the still water. Quiet as they are, they never stop moving. He should also learn from the soaring eagle high in the blue sky. Though it is flying, it does not show much visible body movement.

23、攻人毋太嚴　教人毋過高

攻人之惡，毋太嚴，要思其堪受；教人之善，毋過高，當使其可從。

Don't be too severe in criticizing others. Don't set the goal too high when giving instructions.

Don't be too severe in criticizing people's vice, or it will be difficult for them to accept. Don't set the goal too high when giving people moral instructions, or it will be easy for them to give up.

24、淨從穢生　明從闇出

糞蟲至穢，變為蟬而飲露於秋風；腐草無光，化為螢而翻采於夏月。因知潔常自汙出，明每從晦生也。

The dirty nurture the clean. Obscurity breeds glory.

The white lily is purely clean, but it grows in the dirty soil. The burning fire is gorgeously bright, but it comes from dark black coal. These are the best examples to illustrate that the dirty often nurture the clean, and obscurity breeds glory.

25、客氣伏而正氣伸　妄心殺而真心現

矜高倨傲，無非客氣，降服得客氣下，而後正氣伸；情欲意識，盡屬妄心，消殺得妄心盡，而後真心現。

Suppress bad elements to bring out the good. Get rid of the undue desire to recover heart's original tranquility.

Arrogance and pride are bad elements, which are not native to human nature, so they should be looked upon as intruders. Only when the intruders are suppressed, can a person recover his genuine nature, which is good and virtuous. The undue desire for sensual enjoyment is a frantic indulgence. Only when it is uprooted, can the heart's original tranquility reappear.

26、事悟而癡除　性定而動正

飽後思味，則濃淡之境都消；色後思淫，則男女之見盡絕。故人常以事後之悔悟，破臨事之癡迷，則性定而動無不正。

Experience helps avoid folly. Enlightenment promises proper behavior.

After being sated with food, a person understands that all food tastes alike. After being sated with sex, he realizes that it is nothing interesting. Knowledge and experience help stop further follies.

27、軒冕客志在林泉　山林士胸懷廊廟

居軒冕之中，不可無山林的氣味；處林泉之下，需要懷廊廟的經綸。

People in power should possess little interest in neither worldly fame nor wealth. People out of power should not neglect their duties to the country.

People in power should possess little interest in neither worldly fame nor wealth; otherwise, it will be difficult for them to serve common people honestly. People out of power should keep a close watch on the government and offer constructive suggestions for the welfare of the general public. After all, every person has the responsibility to assist the government to carry out what is beneficial to all walks of life.

28、無過便是功　無怨便是德

處世不必邀功，無過便是功；與人不求感德，無怨便是德。

Doing nothing wrong is praiseworthy. Providing no grounds for complaint is admirable.

People like to be great heroes of great deeds. In fact, doing nothing wrong deserves as much praise. Helping people without asking for credit is a great virtue. However, being fair and honest without giving grounds for complaint is also admirable.

29、做事毋太苦　待人毋太枯

憂勤是美德，太苦則無以適性怡情；澹泊是高風，太枯則無以濟人利物。

Don't work too hard. Don't reject worldly success completely.

Devotion to one's work is commendable. However, working too hard without any fun in life is not healthy both physically and mentally. To value little worldly success is admirable. However, to shun worldly success completely diminishes one's potentiality to serve people.

30、原諒失敗者之初心　注意成功者之末路

事窮勢蹙之人，當原其初心；功成行滿之士，要觀其末路。

Dig the root of a failure. Observe the ending of a success.

Carefully find out a failure's initial intention. That is what really counts. Closely observe a successful man's ending. It is the vital part of a real success.

31、富者應多施捨　智者宜不炫耀

富貴家宜寬厚，而反忌刻，是富貴而貧賤其行矣，如何能享；聰明人宜斂藏，而反炫耀，是聰明而愚懵其病矣，如何不敗。

The rich should give. The wise should not show off.

A mean wealthy person is rich in wealth but poor in character. How can he enjoy good fortune? A boastful intelligent man is gifted in mental capacity but sick with stupidity. How can he be successful?

32、居安思危　處亂思治

居卑而後知登高之為危，處晦而後知向明之太露，守靜而後知好動之過勞，養默而後知多言之為躁。

People usually don't see the danger of a high position until they reach a safe lower spot. People often appreciate law and order only after they have experienced the horror of violence.

People usually don't see the danger of a lofty position until they are in a safe lower spot, don't know the annoyance of being conspicuous until they are cozily unnoticed, don't realize the burden of a busy schedule until they have leisure time, and don't sense the vexation caused by talkativeness until they are peacefully quiet.

33、人能放得心下　即可入聖超凡

放得功名富貴之心下，便可脫凡；放得道德仁義之心下，才可入聖。

The person who can put down the undue desire is great and divine.

The person who can put down the undue desire for wealth and power is extraordinary. The one who can suppress the undue desire for fame is divine.

34、我見害於心　聰明障於道

利欲未盡害心，意見乃害心之蟊賊；聲色未必障道，聰明乃障道之屏藩。

Prejudice is harmful to a person's moral character. The ego is a big obstacle on the way to Tao.

The undue desire for power and wealth is bad for a person's moral character; worse yet is his strong prejudice. The undue desire for sensual pleasure is a big obstacle on the way to living harmoniously with the universe; worse yet is his dreadful ego.

35、知退一步之法　加讓三分之功

人情反覆，世路崎嶇。行不去處，須知退一步之法；行得去處，務加讓三分之功。

Know how to step back and make way for others.

People are fickle and life in this world is rough and harsh. The way to get along with people is same as the way to walk in the street. When the street is so narrow that only one person may pass at a time, retreat a step to let the other one pass first. If the street is quite wide, instead of occupying more than enough, leave plenty room for other people. Thus, many unnecessary conflicts can be avoided.

36、對小人不惡　對君子有禮

待小人，不難於嚴，而難於不惡；待君子，不難於恭，而難於有禮。

Be fair to the petty. Be respectful to the noble.

It is easy to impose harsh discipline on the petty, but difficult to be just and fair. It is easy to be humble and submissive towards the noble, but difficult to be polite and respectful with proper etiquette.

37、留正氣給天地　遺清名於乾坤

寧守渾噩而黜聰明，留些正氣還天地；寧謝紛華而甘澹泊，遺個清名在乾坤。

Preserve the fair and good spirit for the universe. Leave a clean name to the world.

A real person would rather be honest and crude than cunning and artful to preserve the fair and good spirit for the universe, and he would rather live a simple and quiet life than a glorious and splendid one to leave a clean and decent name to the world.

38、伏魔先伏自心　馭橫先平此氣

降魔者先降自心。心伏，則群魔退廳。馭橫者，先馭此氣。氣平，則外橫不侵。

To defeat temptations from outside, defeat inside weakness first. To defeat irrational attacks from outside, be rational inside first.

The worst enemy a person can have is his own weakness. When that is overcome, he can successfully resist any temptations. The worst destructive behavior a person may encounter is his own irrationality. When that is under control, he can be at peace with himself and the world.

39、種田地須除草芟　教弟子嚴謹交遊

教弟子如養閨女，最要嚴出入，謹交遊。若一接近匪人，是清淨田中下一不淨的種子，便終身難植嘉禾矣。

Weeding is necessary while growing plants. Choosing good friends is essential while educating the youth.

Friends are important to everyone. Good friends are great assets to life, but bad ones always cause endless trouble. Since the junior do not have ability to distinguish the good from the bad, it is the responsibility of their elders to keep a close watch for them. The slightest neglect will ruin a junior's whole life.

40、欲路上毋染指　理路上毋退步

欲路上事，毋樂其便而姑為染指，一染指，便深入萬仞。理路上事，毋憚其難而稍為退步，一退步，便遠隔千山。

Avoid the road of desire. Don't retreat from the road of virtue.

The road of desire is easy and merry to travel on, yet one should not enter. One step on it is a step to the bottomless ravine. The road of virtue is hard and rugged, but one should not retreat from it. One step backward is a thousand mountains' distance away from eternal bliss.

41、不流於濃豔　不陷於枯寂

念頭濃者，自待厚，待人亦厚，處處皆厚；念頭淡者，自待薄，待人亦薄，事事皆薄。故君子居常嗜好，不可太濃豔，亦不宜太枯寂。

Be neither wastefully lavish nor harshly stingy.

The generous are generous to both themselves and others. The stingy are hard on both themselves and others. Instead of extremes, a real person's daily life should take the middle way: neither wastefully lavish nor harshly stingy.

42、超越天地之外　不入名利之中

彼富我仁，彼爵我義，君子固不為君相所牢籠；人定勝天，志一動氣，君子亦不受造化之陶鑄。

A real person is not confined to worldly wealth or power. His noble spirit goes above this universe.

Worldly position or wealth will not be able to slave a real person who values only kindness and justice. Neither will destiny be able to confine him, for his noble determination is powerful enough to remold his own destiny.

43、立身要高一步　處世須退一步

立身不高一步立，如塵裡振衣，泥中濯足，如何超達；處世不退一步處，如飛蛾投燭，羝羊觸藩，如何安樂。

Set the life goal a little bit higher. The golden rule of conduct in the world is to compromise.

He who doesn't set life goal a little bit higher is like to dust clothes in the dust and to wash feet in the mud. The outcome can hardly be satisfactory. He who refuses to compromise is like the moth flying to the fire and the antelope entangling its horns in the bushes. The ending is not only unhappy but also unfortunate.

44、修德須忘功名　讀書定要深心

學者要收拾精神，併歸一路。如修德而留意於事功名譽，必無實詣；讀書而寄興於吟詠風雅，定不深心。

To develop moral character, one should disregard worldly success. To pursue profound knowledge, one should not be distracted by vanity.

It is important for a student to concentrate on what he pursues. If he wishes to develop moral character, he should put down undue desires for worldly glory and success, or his pursuit will be doomed to failure. If he wishes to obtain profound knowledge to serve human beings, he should not be distracted by vanity, or his efforts will be futile.

45、真偽之道　只在一念

　　人人有個大慈悲，維摩屠劊無二心也；處處有種真趣味，金屋茅簷非兩地也。只是欲閉情封，當面錯過，便咫尺千里矣。

Good or evil depends on individual choice.

　　Mercy exists in every one's heart. It is in the saint's as well as in the butcher's. Everything has its unique beauty. The golden palace possesses it, so does a thatched cottage. The only reason why people fail to spot the good and beautiful is simply because they are blindfolded by their own selfish desires.

46、道者應有木石心　名相須具雲水趣

　　進德修道，要個木石的念頭，若一有欣羨，便趨欲境；濟世經邦，要段雲水的趣味，若一有貪著，便墮危機。

Possess a heart made of stone or wood to develop moral character. Learn from the flying cloud or the running water to serve people.

　　A stony or wooden heart does not respond to worldly glory or success, and it is exactly what a person who wishes to develop his moral character should have. The flying cloud or the running water does not hoard up anything when it passes through the world, and it is precisely what a person who devotes himself to serving people and his country should learn from.

47、善人和氣一團　惡人殺氣騰騰

吉人無論作用安祥，即夢寐神魂，無非和氣；凶人無論行事狼戾，即聲音笑語，混是殺機。

Kind people are warm and friendly. Vicious people are cold and malicious.

Kind people are peaceful. They impart a warm and friendly atmosphere even in their dreams. Vicious people are cold and cruel. Even their voice and laughter carry malice.

48、欲無禍於昭昭　勿得罪於冥冥

肝受病，則目不能視；腎受病，則耳不能聽。受病於人所不見，必發於人所共見，故君子欲無得禍於昭昭，先無得罪於冥冥。

If a person does not wish to suffer any visible humiliations, he should avoid committing any invisible wrongdoings.

Although inner organs of the physical body are invisible from outside, when they go wrong, the symptoms are bound to show up on the external part of the body. Similarly, a person who does not wish to suffer any humiliations in the open should avoid any evil intentions in the dark.

49、多心招禍　少事為福

福莫福於少事，禍莫禍於多心。唯苦事者，方知少事之為福；唯平心者，始知多心之為禍。

Suspicion invites calamities. Peace beckons blessings.

Peace is the greatest blessing. Suspicion invites calamities. Those who have been in trouble understand the value of peace. Those who have recovered peace realize the horrible harm caused by suspicion.

50、處世要方圓自在　待人要寬嚴得宜

處治世宜方，處亂世宜圓，處叔季之世，當方圓並用；待善人宜寬，待惡人宜嚴，待庸眾之人，當寬嚴互存。

Be flexible to conduct life in the world. Be adjustable to deal with different people.

It is desirable to be square during the time of peace and prosperity, but to be tactful during the war and violence. As in the transitional period, a square-but-tactful attitude is recommended. It is desirable to be kind to good people, but to be strict to the wicked. As to the mediocre, a kind-but-strict attitude is recommended.

51、忘功不忘過　忘怨不忘恩

我有功於人不可念，而過則不可不念；人有恩於我不可忘，而怨則不可不忘。

Forget our favors to others but not faults. Forget people's wrongdoings to us but never a kindness.

Forget any favor we do to others but not any fault we commit. Forget the enmities we bear against others but never the kindness we have received.

52、無求之施一粒萬鍾　有求之施萬金無功

施恩者，內不見己，外不見人，則斗粟可當萬鍾之報；利物者，計己之施，責人之報，雖百鎰難成一文之功。

A small favor without expecting any reward is worth much more than its actual value. A big favor with demand attached loses its significance.

The value of a favor does not depend on its size but on the attitude of the giver. If the giver is self-forgetful and expects nothing for reward, his help though small is priceless. On the contrary, if the giver calculates the value of his assistance and demands a reward, his help though big deserves little praise.

53、推己及人　方便之門

人之際遇，有齊有不齊，而能使己獨齊乎；己之情理，有順有不順，而能使人皆順乎；以此相觀對治，亦是一方便法門。

To stand in another person's shoes is a good way to make rational judgment.

Not a single person in the world can enjoy good fortune or make correct judgment always. We are no exception. It is irrational to ask others to hold the same opinion as ours. To stand back to take a wider perspective or to put ourselves in other people's shoes is a good way to be sensible and make a rational judgment.

54、惡人讀書　適以濟惡

心地乾淨，方可讀書學古。不然，見一善行，竊以濟私，聞一善言，假以覆短，是又藉寇兵，而齎盜糧矣。

Wicked people use knowledge to justify their vice.

Knowledge is power. At a good person's command, it is a powerful force to serve the world. At an evil person's service, it becomes a frightful tool to justify and cover his vice.

55、崇儉養廉　守拙全真

奢者富而不足，何如儉者貧而有餘；能者勞而府怨，何如拙者逸而全真。

Thrift helps promote integrity. Simplicity preserves the genuine happiness in life.

Rich though they are, the extravagant feel inadequate. Poor as they may be, the thrifty have more than enough. Those of great talent take pains to prove their ability but only attract harsh criticism. The simple person keeps things simple and enjoys a peaceful and easy life.

56、讀書希聖講學躬行　居官愛民立業種德

讀書不見聖賢，如鉛槧傭；居官不愛子民，如衣冠盜；講學不尚躬行，為口頭禪；立業不思種德，為眼前花。

The purpose of pursuing knowledge is to become a real person. A teacher should practice what he teaches. The fundamental duty of a government official is to take good care of common people. Only the achievement with solid moral basis will guarantee a long-lasting success.

A student without a lofty purpose is only a copy machine. A government official fails to take good care of common people is a robber in disguise. A teacher does not carry out what he teaches is an advocator of empty words. Any accomplishment without a solid moral basis enjoys a success as short-lived as a flower.

57、讀心中之名文　聽本真之妙曲

人心有一部真文章，都被殘篇斷簡封錮了；有一部真鼓吹，都被妖歌豔舞湮沒了。學者須掃除外物，直覓本來，才有個真受用。

Read the book of conscience. Listen to the music from heart.

Conscience is a sacred book; however, the contents are often distorted by improper excerpts. Heart is a fountain to produce holy music; however, the music is often buried by seductive noise. A truth pursuer should get rid of what is intrusive to recover what is genuine.

58、苦中有樂　樂中有苦

苦心中，常得悅心之趣。得意時，便生失意之悲。

Pleasure exists in misery. Sadness lurks in happiness.

Something pleasing can often be found in a miserable situation. At the peak of happiness, the sad element creeps in.

59、無勝於有德行之行為　無劣於有權力之名譽

富貴名譽，自道德來者，如山林中花，自是舒徐繁衍；自功業來者，如盆檻中花，便有遷徙興廢。若以權力得者，如瓶中花，其根不植，其萎可立而待矣。

Ethical behavior enjoys the highest honor. Power-based reputation suffers the worst condemnation.

Fame and wealth coming from ethical behavior are like flowers in the woods; their flourishing will last forever. Wealth and fame earned from a great accomplishment are similar to flowers in an earthen pot; their glory is undependable. Wealth and fame obtained from power are as flowers in a vase; their decay can be witnessed before long.

60、人死留名　豹死留皮

春至時和，花尚鋪一段好色，鳥且囀幾句好音。士君子幸列頭角，復遇溫飽，不思立好言，行好事，雖是在世百年，恰似未生一日。

Every person wishes to leave behind a good reputation after death. Every leopard wishes to leave behind a magnificent fur.

In the springtime when the weather is mild and pleasant, even flowers offer beautiful colors and birds contribute sweet songs to the world. If a person, fortunate enough to receive good education and enjoy good life, does not do something kind and say something useful, his existence in the world is a complete waste even though his life lasts one hundred years long.

61、寬嚴得宜　勿偏一方

學者有段競業的心思，又要有段瀟灑的趣味。若一味斂束清苦，是有秋殺無春生，何以發育萬物。

Serious purposes and lively interests are equally important.

It is correct that a person should pursue knowledge seriously and make constant improvement, but lively interests are equally important. A person with only serious purposes but without any lively interests is like the earth with only bleak autumn but without vivacious spring. It will be difficult for him to be productive.

62、大智若愚　大巧若拙

真廉無廉名，立名者正所以為貪；大巧無巧術，用術者乃所以為拙。

True wisdom sounds foolish. Great skill looks clumsy.

A person of real integrity does not possess the matching reputation. The one who covets such reputation is greedy. Excellent workmanship does not cut corners. Anyone who does so is truly clumsy.

63、謙虛受益　滿盈招損

欹器[*]以滿覆，撲滿以空全，故君子寧居無不居有，寧處缺不處完。

Modesty gains; arrogance loses.

The container *Qi*[**] overturns when it is full. The piggy bank will not be broken when empty. It is better for a real person to own little than to have plenty, to be improved than to be perfect.

64、名利總墮庸俗　意氣總歸剩技

名根未拔者，縱輕千乘甘一瓢，總墮塵情；客氣未融者，雖澤四海利萬世，終為剩技。

Fame and wealth bend one to be earthly. Arrogance and ego betray one's pettiness.

If a person fails to root out undue desires for fame and wealth, he will eventually become their slave although he claims that he prefers plain and simple life. If a person fails to expel his arrogance and ego, he is destined to be a petty man although his kindness reaches millions of people and lasts millions of years.

---

[*] 欹器：中空時傾向一側，注水一半時則直立，大滿時傾覆。古代置於君王之側，作為謙戒之器。

[**] *Qi*: An object that leans when empty, overturns when brimming, and stands upright when only half filled. It used to be placed on the Chinese emperor's side to remind him to be humble.

65、心地須要光明　念頭不可暗昧

心體光明，暗室中有青天；念頭暗昧，白日下有厲鬼。

Be fair and honest. Keep the thought unpolluted.

When there is justice in heart, light can be found even in a dark room. When the thought is polluted, there are devils even under the bright sun.

66、勿羨貴顯　勿憂飢餓

人知名位為樂，不知無名位之樂為真；人知飢寒為憂，不知不飢不寒之憂為更甚。

Don't envy the powerful or wealthy. Don't worry about poverty.

People assume that happiness is being powerful and wealthy. They don't realize that the happiness of being ordinary is more enjoyable. People suppose that poverty causes anxiety. They don't know that those who possess abundant have greater worries.

67、陰惡之惡大　顯善之善小

為惡而畏人知，惡中猶有善路；為善而急人知，善處即是惡根。

The covered evil is most dangerous. A publicized good diminishes its value.

There is hope for the person who feels ashamed of his evil behavior. A good deed turns sour as soon as the person tries hard to publicize it.

68、君子居安思危　天亦無用其伎

天之機緘不測，抑而伸，伸而抑，皆是播弄英雄，顛倒豪傑處。君子只是逆來順受，居安思危，天亦無

Destiny is powerless over the one who makes hay while the sun shines.

Destiny is unpredictable and is famous for tricks. If a person meets adversity submissively and makes hay while the sun shines; destiny, trickery as it is, is powerless over him.

69、中和為福　偏激為災

　　燥性者火熾，遇物則焚；寡恩者冰清，逢物必殺；凝滯固執者，如死水腐木，生機已絕。俱難建功業而延福祉。

The moderate are blessed. Extremes lead to disaster.

　　A hot-tempered person is easily angered. His anger burns everything he touches. A cold person has no mercy. Anyone who is against him is destroyed. An obstinate person is like the stagnant water or the rotten tree, where no life can be found. These three types of persons are difficult to have a successful present, not to mention a happy future.

70、多喜養福　去殺遠禍

　　福不可徼，養喜神，以為召福之本；禍不可避，去殺機，以為遠禍之方。

Cheerfulness breeds good fortune. Evil intentions brew disasters.

　　Good fortune cannot be forced. Cheerfulness breeds good fortune. Misfortune is hard to avoid. Shake off evil intentions to guard against disasters.

71、謹言慎行　君子之道

十語九中，未必稱奇，一語不中，則衍尤駢集；十謀九成，未必歸功，一謀不成，則訾議叢興。君子所以寧默毋躁，寧拙無巧。

A real person should be careful of both his words and his behavior.

Of ten predictions, nine are accurate, the clever predictor may not be admired for the accurate nine; but it is sure that he will get a lot of blame for the missed one. Of ten plans, nine are successful, the smart planner may not win any credit for the successful nine; however, it can be counted on that he will get a great amount of criticism for the failed one. That is why a real person would rather be quiet than talkative, and crude than skilful.

72、殺氣寒薄　和氣福厚

天地之氣，暖則生，寒則殺，故性氣冷清者，受享亦涼薄；唯和氣熱心之人，其福亦厚，其澤亦長。

Indifference is cold and barren. Geniality is warm and abundant.

When the weather is warm, everything on the earth thrives. When it turns cold, all wither. For the same reason, a warm and friendly person enjoys abundant and long-lasting blessings, while the cold and indifferent one has little chance to enjoy any really good fortune.

73、正義路廣　欲情道窄

天理路上甚寬，稍遊心，胸中便覺廣大宏朗；人欲路上甚窄，才寄跡，眼前俱是荊棘泥塗。

The road of righteousness is broad. The road of desire is narrow.

The road of righteousness is broad and bright. Any person travels on it feels carefree and finds the prospect bright and rosy. The road of desire is narrow and rough. Any person walks on it encounters only thorns and mud, and he finds his prospect dark and bleak.

74、磨練之福久　參勘之知真

一苦一樂相磨練，練極而成福者，其福始久；一疑一信相參勘，勘極而成知者，其知始真。

Blessings obtained after numerous hardships last long. Knowledge gained after much deliberation is real.

Blessings obtained after numerous hardships last long. Knowledge gained after much deliberation and many tests is real.

75、虛心明義理　實心卻物欲

心不可不虛，虛則義理來居；心不可不實，實則物欲不入。

Empty the heart to make room for moral teachings. Stuff the heart with upright principles to ward off improper desires.

In pursuing moral teachings, one should be humble. To empty the heart to make room as large as possible for good teachings is important. To ward off undue desires, one should be firm. To stuff the heart with whatever is righteous so that undue desires cannot find any room there is necessary.

76、厚德載物　雅量容人

地之穢者多生物，水之清者常無魚，故君子常存含垢納汙之量，不可操好潔獨行之操。

Genuine kindness discriminates against none. True tolerance accepts differences.

Earth rich in fertilizers grows abundant lives. Water extremely pure with absolutely no microbes supports no fish. A real person should discriminate against no one and should tolerate differences. He should especially not isolate himself from other people to distinguish his purity.

77、憂勞興國　逸欲亡身

泛駕之馬可就馳驅，躍冶之金終歸型範，只一優遊不振，便終身無個進步。白沙*云：「為人多病未足羞，一生無病是吾憂。」真確論也。

Tough times and hard work help build a strong and prosperous country. Comfortable life and jolly amusements ruin a person's life.

A wild horse can be tamed to serve humans. Scattered gold drops can be tampered into useful shapes. Any person without a life goal will never make any progress. The famous scholar Mr. Bai Sha (1428-1500) said: "Having millions of faults is nothing to be ashamed of. Having absolutely no fault worries me a great deal." What a wise saying it is!

78、一念貪私　萬劫不復

人只一念貪私，便銷剛為柔，塞智為昏，變恩為慘，染潔為汙，壞了一生人品。故古人以不貪為寶，所以度越一世。

The slightest touch of avarice leads a person to an eternal fall.

The slightest touch of avarice can transform the strong into the submissive, the wise into the foolish, the kind into the cruel, and the clean into the filthy. A lifelong splendid reputation may thus be spoiled. Great people of old times have won the public's lasting respect by restraining themselves from avarice.

---

* 白沙（1428-1500）：原名陳獻章，明代理學家，居廣東新會縣白沙鄉，門人稱白沙先生。

79、心公不昧　六賊無蹤

耳目見聞為外賊，情欲意識為內賊，只是主人翁惺惺不昧，獨坐中堂，賊便化為家人矣。

If the master of the heart does not doze, the six thieves fail to cause mischief.

What we see and what we hear are the thieves from outside. Our undue desires are the thieves from inside. Combined together they are six thieves from six senses: color (eyes), sound (ears), smell (nose), taste (tongue), sense of touch (body), and emotion (heart). These six thieves never give up any chance to seduce their master. However, if the master is in constant vigilance, these thieves can be reformed into family members who will assist their master to do what is positive instead of what is negative.

80、勉勵現前之業　圖謀未來之功

圖未就之功，不如保已成之業；悔既往之失，不如防將來之非。

Work hard on the present achievement to ensure a bright future.

It is better to work hard on what is already accomplished than to dream for what is uncertain. It is better to take precautions against future mistakes than to regret what is already past.

81、養天地正氣　法古今完人

氣象要高曠，而不可疏狂；心思要縝密，而不可瑣屑；趣味要沖淡，而不可偏枯；操守要嚴明，而不可激烈。

Cultivate the upright qualities of the universe. Follow the examples of real people of the present and the past.

Life's goal should be lofty but not wild. Thoughts should be carefully reviewed but not petty. Interests should be light but not barren. Behavior should be honest but not stiff.

82、不著色相　不留聲影

風來疏竹，風過而竹不留聲；雁度寒潭，雁去而潭不留影。故君子事來而心始現，事去而心隨空。

Keep neither image nor sound.

Bamboo bushes cease making any sound after the wind has passed through. The lake does not keep their images after wild geese have flown over. A real person's mind is like the bamboo and the lake. It acts accordingly to what is happening, but resumes its peaceful state as soon as the event is over.

83、君子德行　其道中庸

清能有容，仁能善斷，明不傷察，直不過矯，是謂蜜餞不甜，海味不鹹，才是懿德。

A real person's behavior never goes to extremes.

A real person is clean and honest but can tolerate people's faults, kind but is able to judge the right from the wrong, careful but not fastidious, and upright but not stiff. True ethical behavior should be like the tasty preserved fruits that are not overly sweet, and like the delicious seafood that is not extremely salty.

84、君子窮當益工　勿失風雅氣度

貧家淨掃地，貧女淨梳頭，景色雖不豔麗，氣度自是風雅，士君子一當窮愁寥落，奈何輒自廢弛哉。

Redouble efforts to reach the goal during times of adversity. Lose neither confidence nor dignity.

A poor family kept clean is like a poor lady kept well-groomed. Neither is magnificent, but both are graceful. How can an educated person toss away his confidence and dignity in times of adversity?

85、未雨綢繆　有備無患

閒中不放過，忙處有受用；靜中不落空，動處有受用；暗中不欺隱，明處有受用。

Prepare for the rain before it comes. There will be no danger when there is adequate preparation.

If a person does not idle away his leisure time, he will harvest the benefit when busy. If a person never stops improving himself while at peace, he will be able to meet the unexpected challenge with ease. If a person refuses to deceive in the dark, he will be richly rewarded in the open.

86、懸崖勒馬　起死回生

念頭起處，才覺向欲路上去，便挽從理路上來。一起便覺，一覺便轉，此是轉禍為福，起死回生的關頭，切莫輕易放過。

To rein in the horse at the edge of a cliff is to save life from mortal danger.

To stop an undue desire at the very beginning of its occurrence is to reverse disaster to good fortune. Be alert to any undue desire and don't hesitate to correct it as soon as it is detected. The crucial turning point from death to life should not be neglected.

87、寧靜淡泊　觀心之道

　　靜中念慮澄徹，見心之真體；閒中氣象從容，識心之真機；淡中意趣沖夷，得心之真味。觀心證道，無如此三者。

The best way to understand one's own heart is when serene without any undue desire.

　　Being free from anxiety is the real nature of the heart. It can be found only when the person is calm and serene. Being relaxed is the real spirit of the heart. It can be found only when the person is not busily engaged. Being peaceful is the real joy of the heart. It can be found only when the person is without any undue desire. Serenity, leisure time, and light desire are three effective ways to find and understand the truth of one's own heart.

88、動中靜是真靜　苦中樂見真樂

　　靜中靜非真靜，動處靜得來，才是性天之真境；樂處樂非真樂，苦中樂得來，才是心體之真機。

To be composed in turmoil . To stay joyful in hardship.

　　It is easy to be composed in a peaceful situation, but it takes real strength to be composed in turmoil. It is easy to be joyful in good fortune, but it takes true wisdom to stay joyful in hardship.

89、捨己毋處疑　施恩毋望報

捨己毋處其疑，處其疑，即所捨之志多愧矣；施人毋責其報，責其報，併所施之心俱非矣。

Make sacrifices without hesitation. Perform good deeds without expecting a reward.

Don't hesitate to make sacrifices. Hesitation disgraces the honorable intention. Don't expect any reward for a good act. Expectation degrades good will.

90、厚德以積福　逸心以補勞　修道以解阨

天薄我以福，吾厚吾德以迓之；天勞我以形，吾逸吾心以補之；天阨我以遇，吾亨吾道以通之。天且奈我何哉。

Accumulate good deeds to increase chances for good fortune, suppress undue desires to ease physical and mental fatigue, and behave conscientiously to shun misfortune.

Any person who accumulates good deeds to increase the meager blessings Heaven grants him, suppresses undue desires to ease the physical and mental fatigue Fate imposes on him, and behaves conscientiously to overcome the hard lot God assigns to him is able to mold his own destiny.

91、天福無欲之貞士 而禍避禍之憸人

貞士無意徼福，天即就無心處牖其衷；憸人著意避禍，天即就著意中奪其魄。可見天之機權最神，人之智巧何益。

God blesses those who don't pursue personal profit but condemns those who shun personal loss.

God blesses those who don't seek personal profit but condemns those who shun personal loss. In front of God, human wisdom is useless.

92、人生重結果 種田看收成

聲妓晚景從良，一世之煙花無礙；貞婦白頭失守，半生之清苦俱非。語云：看人只看後半截，真良言也。

The final ending is what counts in a person's life. The harvest is what matters in planting.

If a lustful prostitute becomes a virtuous housewife even at a very late age, her infamous past is forgiven. When a virtuous lady indulges herself in immoral conduct towards the end of her life, her sparkling life history is ruined. It is true that in judging a person only the latter part of his life is significant.

93、多種功德　勿貪權位

平民肯種德施惠，便是無位的公相；士夫徒貪權市寵，竟成有爵的乞人。

Be diligent in doing what is good and kind. Be greedy for neither power nor wealth.

A common citizen, diligent in doing what is good and kind, is a nobleman without a title. A high-ranking official, greedy for power and wealth, is a beggar with a noble name.

94、當念積累之難　常思傾覆之易

問祖宗之德澤，吾身所享者是，當念其積累之難；問子孫之福祉，吾身所貽者是，要思其傾覆之易。

It is difficult to build but easy to destroy.

We should never forget the hardship our ancestors have gone through to build what we enjoy now. We should always keep in mind that the accomplishment we wish to pass on to our descendants are easy to destroy.

95、只畏偽君子　不怕真小人

君子而詐善，無異小人之肆惡；君子而改節，不及小人之自新。

Hypocrites are dreadful, but not necessary the infamous.

There is no difference between a hypocrite and an infamous evil person. A repentant sinner is better than a saint who decides to sell his soul to the devil in the end.

96、春風解凍　和氣消冰

家人有過，不宜暴怒，不宜輕棄；此事難言，借他事隱諷之；今日不悟，俟來日再警之。如春風解凍，如和氣消冰，才是家庭的型範。

Spring wind thaws frozen earth. Geniality dissolves an icy atmosphere.

It is not proper to be angry with or to reject our family members when they commit something wrong. Instead, it is advisable to offer them either direct advice or indirect hints to help them. If our efforts fail to show any favorable result, wait for a proper moment to try again in the future. Spring wind will eventually thaw the frozen earth, and geniality will sooner or later dissolve an icy atmosphere. These two examples serve good models for us to follow.

97、能徹見心性　則天下平穩

此心常看得圓滿，天下自無缺陷之世界；此心常放得寬平，天下自無險側之人情。

Sincerity, generosity, and justice lead to a peaceful and happy world.

Positive attitude will be rewarded with a positive world, sincerity, generosity, and justice, put a stop to treachery.

98、操履不可少變　鋒芒不可太露

澹泊之士，必為濃艷者所疑；檢飾之人，多為放肆者所忌。君子處此，固不可稍變其操履，亦不可露其鋒芒。

Don't bend principles. Don't flaunt fine qualities.

A person who is indifferent to power and wealth will certainly cause suspicion among the ambitious. A well-behaved person often attracts hostility from the dissipated. In facing suspicion and hostility, a real person neither bends his principles nor flaunts his fine qualities.

99、順境不足喜　逆境不足憂

居逆境中，周身皆鍼砭藥石，砥節勵行而不覺；處順境內，眼前盡兵刃戈矛，銷膏靡骨而不知。

Don't be exultant in prosperity. Don't be depressed in adversity.

In a time of adversity, one learns useful lessons from difficulties without notice. In a happy time, people are not aware that they are nibbled away by the invisible devils disguised in all kinds of comforts and enjoyments around him.

100、富貴而恣勢弄權　乃自取滅亡之道

生長富貴叢中的，嗜欲如猛火，權勢似烈燄。若不帶些清冷氣味，其火燄若不焚人，必將自爍矣。

When the wealthy and powerful abuse their privileges, they are digging their own graves.

Those who are brought up in powerful and wealthy families often indulge heavily in undue desires. The fire-like desires and the red-hot wealth and power if not properly curbed, will certainly incinerate their masters if not burn the people around.

101、精誠所感　金石為開

人心一真，便霜可飛，城可隕，金石可鏤。若偽妄之人，形骸徒具，真宰已亡，對人面目可憎，獨居則形影自愧。

Even an unyielding rock can be moved by sincerity.

Sincerity can cause frost in June, bring down a sturdy city wall, and enable unyielding rock and gold to be carved. An insincere person, though he possesses a human form, has lost his precious soul. He is disgusted by all when with people, and is ashamed of himself when alone.

102、文章極處無奇巧　人品極處則本然

文章做到極處，無有他奇，只是恰好；人品做到極處，無有他異，只是本然。

An excellent piece of writing does not need special skills. The best character is without any fancy adornment.

There is nothing special about an excellent piece of writing. Being proper is the only secret. There is nothing unusual about an excellent character. Staying in its genuine state is the only requirement.

103、明世相之本體　負天下之重任

以幻跡言，無論功名富貴，即肢體亦屬委形。以真境言，無論父母兄弟，即萬物皆吾一體。人能看得破，認得真，才可以任天下之負擔，亦可脫世間之韁鎖。

Distinguish reality from illusion. Take on important responsibilities to serve the world.

With regard to illusion, everything from fame and wealth to our physical bodies are but temporary phenomenon; while in reality, not only our nuclear family but also everything in the universe is an essential part of our being. After achieving the ability to distinguish these two, one is capable of taking on important responsibilities to serve the world, while at the same time, being free from worldly bondage.

104、凡事當留餘地　五分便無殃悔

爽口之味，皆爛腸腐骨之藥，五分便無殃；快心之事，悉敗身喪德之媒，五分便無悔。

Don't go to extremes. Moderation prevents misfortune and regrets.

Most delicious foods are bad for health. Taking only half of our actual needs will keep us safe from harm. Enjoyable activities often lead to destruction. Refraining from heavy indulgence prevents regrets and misfortune.

105、忠恕待人　養德遠害

不責人小過，不發人陰私，不念人舊惡，三者可以養德，亦可以遠害。

Forgiveness and trustiness are effective ways to cultivate a good character and keep troubles away.

Don't punish people for their negligence, publicize their secrets, or keep in mind old enmities. These three principles help us cultivate a good moral character and keep us away from troubles.

106、持身不可輕　用心不可重

士君子持身不可輕，輕則物能撓我，而無悠閒鎮定之趣；用意不可重，重則我為物泥，而無瀟灑活潑之機。

Behave with dignity. Possess no strong passions.

A real person shouldn't look down on himself, or he is easily influenced by others and thereby ill at ease with himself and loses his calm and tranquility. A real person shouldn't possess strong passions either, or he is easily bound and thereby loses his vitality and vigor.

107、人生無常　不可虛度

天地有萬古，此身不再得；人生只百年，此日最易過。幸生其間者，不可不知有生之樂，亦不可不懷虛生之憂。

Life is not eternal. Don't waste it.

The universe lasts forever, but not human life, which lasts only a swift hundred years and will never be repeated again. He who is lucky enough to live in this world should enjoy life, but at the same time should also do something meaningful not to waste such a precious existence.

108、德怨兩忘　恩仇俱泯

怨因德彰，故使人德我，不若德怨之兩忘；仇因恩立，故使人知恩，不若恩仇之俱泯。

Remember neither favors nor enmity. Forget both hostility and kindness.

When kindness fails to win gratitude and favors fail to reap rewards, enmity and hostility come to our heart. To avoid the unhappy results, it is better to forget completely the kindness and favors we have given to people. After all, true kindness does not ask for gratitude, and sincere help does not demand any rewards.

109、持盈履滿　君子兢兢

老來疾病，都是壯時招的；衰後罪孽，都是盛時造的。故持盈履滿，君子尤兢兢焉。

Be careful when in the glory of success.

The disease of old age is the result of negligence caused when young. The distress suffered in a downfall is brought about by the vices committed when in the glory of success. This is why people should be especially careful when everything in the garden is rosy and lovely.

110、卻私扶公　修身種德

市私恩，不如扶公議；結新知，不如敦舊好；立榮名，不如種隱德；尚奇節，不如謹庸行。

Support public justice but not personal favors.
Cultivate good character and accumulate good deeds.

To support public justice is better than to seek personal favors. To restore old friendships is better than to develop a new. To quietly perform what is ethical is better than to build a fabulous fame. To live an ordinary peaceful life is better than to be extraordinary and glorious.

111、勿犯公論　勿諂權門

公平正論，不可犯手，一犯，則貽羞萬世；權門私竇，不可著腳，一著，則沾汙終身。

Don't offend against fair public opinion. Don't flatter the powerful.

Don't offend against fair public opinion, or the infamy will last millions of years. Don't flatter the powerful, or the stain will stay all your life.

112、直躬不畏人忌　無惡不懼人毀

曲意而使人喜，不若直躬而使人忌；無善而使人譽，不若無惡而致人毀。

Integrity fears no bitter feelings. Moral excellence fears no slanders.

It is better to be disliked because of integrity than to bend to please. It is better to be hurt by unfounded slanders than to be rewarded for undeserved credit.

113、從容處家族之變　剴切規朋友之失

處父兄骨肉之變，宜從容，不宜激烈；遇朋友交遊之失，宜剴切，不宜優遊。

Be composed in facing family conflicts. Be sincere about a friend's mistake.

Instead of taking drastic means to solve family conflicts, it is better to face it in a composed manner. Instead of overlooking a friend's mistake, it is better to point it out sincerely.

114、大處著眼　小處著手

小處不滲漏，暗處不欺隱，末路不怠荒，才是個真正英雄。

Be farsighted, but begin with the very fundamental.

A true hero does not neglect small details, cheat in the dark, or give up in time of distress.

115、愛重反為仇　薄極反成喜

千金難結一時之歡，一飯竟致終身之感；蓋愛重反為仇，薄極反成喜也。

Strong passions evolve into hostility. Insignificant but timely assistance results in great joy.

Often where millions of dollars fail, a simple meal succeeds. Strong passions often evolve into hostility, but insignificant but timely assistance results in great joy.

116、藏巧於拙　寓清於濁

藏巧於拙，用晦而明；寓清於濁，以屈為伸；真涉世之一壺，藏身之三窟也。

Hide ingenuity behind crudeness. Conceal purity in muddiness.

To hide ingenuity behind crudeness, to use obscurity to protect brightness, to conceal purity in muddiness, and to bend in order to stretch are golden rules to conduct life in the world.

117、盛極必衰　剝極必復

衰颯的景象，就在盛滿中；發生的機緘，即在零落內。故君子居安，宜操一心以慮患；處變，當堅百忍以圖成。

The peak of prosperity foretells decline. The ultimate end of despair is hope.

The decline lurks in prosperity, and a new life exists in ruins. While in good fortune, be prepared for the unexpected blow. While in distress, be patient for the arrival of success.

118、奇異無遠識　獨行無恆操

驚奇喜異者，無遠大之識。苦節獨行者，非恆久之操。

Novelty wears off soon. Austerity does not last long.

He who likes novelty does not have a long term perspective; those who live in abnormal austerity do not last long.

119、放下屠刀　立地成佛

當怒火慾水正騰沸處，明明知得，又明明犯著，知的是誰，犯的又是誰。此處能猛然轉念，邪魔便為真君矣。

Put down the butcher's knife to become Buddha at once.

People are blind to neither right nor wrong even in their furious rage or when they are overcome by the strongest passion. However, they often yield to what is wrong. At that decisive moment, if they can turn back, even though they are as vicious as devils, they can become as holy as saints instantly.

120、毋偏信自任　毋自滿嫉人

毋偏信而為奸所欺，毋自任而為氣所使，毋以己之長而形人之短，毋因己之拙而忌人之能。

Don't listen to only one side of the story nor be obstinate. Be neither self-conceited nor jealous of other people.

Listening to only one side of the story can easily be deceived by the wicked. Being irrationally obstinate is easy to be controlled by emotions. Don't expose other people's weakness by flaunting our own strength. Don't be jealous of those whose ability surpasses ours.

121、毋以短攻短　毋以頑濟頑

人之短處，要曲為彌縫，如暴而揚之，是以短攻短；人有頑固，要善為化誨，如忿而疾之，是以頑濟頑。

Don't attack people's shortcomings. Don't be headstrong towards the stubborn.

By exposing, instead of concealing, other people's shortcomings, we expose our own weakness. To be angry with the stubborn, instead of guiding them patiently, we put ourselves on their level.

122、對陰險者勿推心　遇高傲者勿多口

遇沉沉不語之士，且莫輸心；見悻悻自好之人，應須防口。

Be reserved towards the sneaky. Be quiet with the proud.

Don't trust the one who is sneaky. Close mouth when with the one who is proud and self-conceited.

123、震聾啟瞶　臨深履薄

念頭昏散處，要知提醒；念頭吃緊時，要知放下。不然恐去昏昏之病，又來憧憧之擾矣。

Use the deafening sound to make the deaf hear. Use the blinding light to make the blind see. Act prudently as at the edge of a high cliff and as on the surface of the thin ice.

When a person becomes drowsy in time of peace, it is important to remind him to be alert. When a person is anxious in time of adversity, it is important to remind him to be calm. Neither drowsiness nor anxiety is good for a person.

124、君子之心　雨過天晴

霽日青天，倏變為迅雷震電；疾風怒雨，倏轉為朗月晴空。氣機何嘗一毫凝滯，太虛何嘗一毫障塞，人之心體，亦當如是。

A real person's conscience is as clear as the sky after a storm.

A sunny fine day suddenly changes into thunder and lightning. In a twinkling of time, strong gusts of wind and pouring rain are transformed into a tranquil night with a bright moon in the sky. In the universe, the motion of air never ceases and nothing can block its way. A real person's conscience, like the air in the universe, should be always on the go and is never hindered by anything.

125、有識有力　魔鬼無蹤

勝私制欲之功，有曰識不早力不易者，有曰識得破忍不過者。蓋識是一顆照魔的明珠，力是一把斬魔的慧劍，兩者不可少也。

Devils shun those who possess wisdom and determination.

Why a person is unable to defeat undue desires and selfishness? Some people fail to spot them in time and miss the chance. Some spot them in time but are weak in will-power to defeat them. Wisdom is a bright pearl to reveal evil, and determination is a precious sword to slay devils. Both are indispensable to reach the goal of defeating undue desires and selfishness.

126、大量能容　不動聲色

覺人之詐，不形於言；受人之侮，不動於色。此中有無窮意味，亦有無窮受用。

True forbearance shows no signs of unhappiness.

Those who keep silence after being deceived and show no indignation after being insulted understand the essence of true forbearance and will be able to enjoy its boundless benefits.

127、困苦窮乏　鍛鍊身心

橫逆困窮是鍛鍊豪傑的一副爐鎚。受其鍛鍊，則身心交益；不受其鍛鍊，則身心交損。

Poverty and adversity help develop mind and body.

Poverty and adversity are the anvil and the hammer to mold heroes. The person who has the courage to accept their challenges will benefit from them. If not, he will deteriorate in both mind and body.

128、人乃天地之縮圖　天地乃人之父母

吾身一小天地也，使喜怒不愆，好惡有則，便是燮理的功夫；天地一大父母也，使民無怨諮，物無氛疹，亦是敦睦的氣象。

A person is a microcosm of the universe. Heaven and Earth are the parents of all beings.

A person is a microcosm of the universe. If a person's emotions and conduct are properly controlled and guided, he may live happily in peace. Heaven and Earth are parents of all creation in the universe. If they oversee and protect the earth with justice and kindness, they provide peace and harmony for all.

129、戒疏於慮　警傷於察

害人之心不可有，防人之心不可無，此戒疏於慮也；寧受人之欺，毋逆人之詐，此儆傷於察也。二語並存，精明而渾厚矣。

Both vigilance and trusting are important.

People should be vigilant. Intentions to hurt other people are forbidden, but precautions against potential malice are necessary. People should be trusting. Without good grounds to be suspicious of others is deviant and oversensitive. Those who know the importance of vigilance and trusting are wise and kind.

130、辨別是非　認識大體

毋因群疑而阻獨見，毋任己意而廢人言，毋私小惠而傷大體，毋借公論以快私情。

Distinguish right from wrong. Recognize the public interests.

Don't abandon sound personal opinion because of widespread unfavorable criticism. Don't turn down a good suggestion by reason of personal prejudice. Don't damage the public interests for individual profit. Don't attack private enemies by exploiting public opinion.

131、親近善人須知幾杜讒　剷除惡人應保密防禍

善人未能急親，不宜預揚，恐來讒詐之奸；惡人未能輕去，不宜先發，恐遭媒孽之禍。

Develop friendship with the virtuous gradually to prevent slanders. Remove the vicious on the quiet to guard against danger.

Develop friendship with the virtuous gradually without publicity to prevent possible slanders. Remove the vicious quietly with thorough preparations to prevent potential malicious revenge.

132、節義來自暗室不欺　經綸繰出臨深履薄

青天白日的節義，自暗室漏屋中培來；旋乾轉坤的經綸，自臨深履薄處繰出。

Integrity is to behave honestly even in adversity. The great history-changing theory comes from much deliberation while confronting menacing dangers.

The spotless noble character is cultivated in adversity. The great history-changing theory is formed by much deliberation while confronting menacing dangers.

133、倫常本乎天性　不可任德懷恩

父慈子孝，兄友弟恭，縱做到極處，俱是合當如此，著不得一絲感激的念頭。如施者任德，受者懷恩，便是路人，便是市道矣。

It is human nature for family members to love each other. It is not proper for them to show off kindness or to express gratitude to each other.

Parental love, filial piety, and friendly relations among siblings are all human nature. It is not proper for family members to show off their kindness or to express gratitude to each other. In doing so, family members become only strangers, and family relationships but business contracts.

134、不誇妍好潔　無醜汙之辱

有妍必有醜為之對，我不誇妍，誰能醜我；有潔必有汙為之仇，我不好潔，誰能汙我。

Boast not of your virtue, and you will not be accused of evil.

Everything has two sides, and every action has an equal and opposite reaction. He who is humble enough not to boast of his virtue, people will not accuse him of evil.

135、富貴多炎涼　骨肉多妒忌

炎涼之態，富貴更甚於貧賤；妒忌之心，骨肉尤狠於外人。此處若不當以冷腸，禦以平氣，鮮不日坐煩惱障中矣。

Most wealthy and powerful people are snobbish. Family members are inclined to be jealous of each other.

It is more often for the rich and powerful to be snobbish than those who are poor and common. It is much easier for family members to be jealous of each other than those who are mere acquaintances. If people fail to stay cool and calm to face the unpleasant situations, troubles will be like shadows never leaving them alone.

136、功過不可少混　恩仇不可過明

功過不容少混，混則人懷惰墮之心；恩仇不可太明，明則人起攜貳之志。

Don't confusingly mix rewards with penalties. Don't distinctively distinguish favorites from those who are not.

People will be lazy and slack if we fail to draw a clear line between rewards and penalties. People will be discouraged and give up if we distinctively separate those who are our favorites from those who are not.

137、位盛危至　德高謗興

爵位不宜太盛，太盛則危；能事不宜盡畢，盡畢則衰；行誼不宜過高，過高則謗興而毀來。

High position attracts danger. Conceited lofty conduct invites slander.

When the position is too high, it attracts danger. When the ability is used up, it is on the decline. When the conduct is conceitedly lofty, it invites slander.

138、陰惡禍深　陽善功小

惡忌陰，善忌陽。故惡之顯者禍淺，而隱者禍深；善之顯者功小，而隱者功大。

The harm caused by a concealed evil is big. The merit of a publicized virtue is small.

An exposed evil causes less harm than a concealed one. A covered virtue is more admirable than the publicized one.

139、應以德馭才　勿恃才收德

德者才之主，才者德之奴；有才無德，如家無主而奴用事矣，幾何不魍魎倡狂。

Ability should be under the guidance of virtue, or the result will be deplorable.

Virtue is the master of ability while ability is at the service of virtue. When the ability is without the guidance of virtue, it is like a house without a master. When a house is under the management of servants without the supervision of a master, how can people expect it to be prosperous and orderly?

140、窮寇勿追　投鼠忌器

鋤奸杜倖，要放他一條去路。若使之一無所容，譬如塞鼠穴者，一切去路都塞盡，則一切好物俱咬破矣。

Don't chase after a wicked person to the wall. Consider the value of the object when you throw it at a mouse.

It is better to leave a mouse hole open for the mouse to run away because when the mouse fails to find an escape, it will damage everything valuable in the room. For the same reason, it is better to give the wicked person a chance to repent than to chase after him to the end of the road.

141、過歸己任　功讓他人

當與人同過，不當與人同功，同功則相忌；可與人共患難，不可與人共安樂，共樂則相仇。

Take the blame, but yield the credit to others.

Share blame not credit. Sharing credit causes hostility. Share the hardship in adversity not the comforts in easy life. Sharing comforts creates enemies.

142、警世救人　功德無量

士君子，貧不能濟物者，遇人癡迷處，出一言提醒之，遇人急難處，出一言解救之，亦是無量功德。

Offering useful advice is the best kind of help.

If a person cannot help people materially, his kindness is beyond measure as well when he gives useful advice to those who are either in foolish indulgence or in great difficulty.

143、趨炎附勢　人情之常

飢則附，飽則颺，燠則趨，寒則棄，人情之通患也。

It is human nature to flatter those who are wealthy and powerful.

It is human nature for hungry people to flatter the person who has abundant food and leave him when they are sated. It is human nature for profit-hunters to cajole the person who is hot with power and money and desert him when he is cold with nothing attractive left.

144、須冷眼觀物　勿輕動剛腸

君子宜淨拭冷眼，慎勿輕動剛腸。

Observe objectively. Make decisions carefully.

A real person should always observe objectively and never make a decision carelessly.

145、量弘識高　功德日進

德隨量進，量由識長。故欲厚其德，不可不弘其量。欲弘其量，不可不大其識。

Increasing both knowledge and the capacity of tolerance is the best way to develop moral character.

Moral character develops in proportion with the capacity of tolerance, which is increased with the help of knowledge. One who wishes to develop moral character has to first accumulate his knowledge, which is an essential factor to increase his capacity of tolerance.

146、人心惟危　道心惟微

一燈螢然，萬籟無聲，此吾人初入冥寂時也；曉夢初醒，群動未起，此吾人初出混沌處也。乘此而一念迴光，炯然反照，始知耳目口鼻皆桎梏，而情欲嗜好悉機械矣。

Human desires are dangerous. The way to universal harmony is subtle.

Late at night when the earth is quietly at rest, human nature retreats back to its original state. Early in the morning when the universe is just about to start its daily activity, human nature is fresh with its original features. Those are the best moments for a person exploring his genuine nature to find the way to universal harmony. He will find that sensual pleasures keep him in bondage and undue desires keep him trapped.

147、諸惡莫作　眾善奉行

反己者，觸事皆成藥石；尤人者，動念即是戈矛。一以闢眾善之路，一以濬諸惡之源，相去天壤矣。

Avoid all vices. Follow all virtues.

A person who constantly examines himself for improvement finds that every single event is valuable to help him become better. The person who always puts the blame on others equips his every single motive with hostility. The former opens the road to great virtues; the latter enlarges the source for vices. The difference between these two cannot be calculated.

148、功名一時　氣節千載

事業文章隨身銷毀，而精神萬古如新；功名富貴逐世轉移，而氣節千載一日。君子信不當以彼易此也。

Fame and material achievements are temporary, but ethical behavior lasts forever.

A person's material achievements end with his death, but his spirit persists. A person's fame and wealth are subject to change with time, but his ethical behavior lasts forever. Will a wise person trade the immortal for the temporal?

149、自然造化之妙　智巧所不能及

魚網之設，鴻則罹其中。螳螂之貪，雀又乘其後。機裡藏機，變外生變，智巧何足恃哉。

The ingenuity of Heaven is beyond the greatest wisdom and the best skill on earth.

The fishing net may catch wild geese instead of fish. A bird is right at the back of the greedy mantis that is concentrating on catching a cicada. There are tricks in the trick and changes in the middle of change. Human wisdom and skill are not dependable.

150、真誠為人　圓轉涉世

作人無點真誠念頭，便成個花子，事事皆虛；涉世無段圓活機趣，便是個木人，處處有礙。

Be sincere but flexible.

A person should be sincere and honest, or he is only a paper figure to whom nothing is real. A person should be flexible and lively, or he is but a wooden dummy to whom everything is an obstacle.

151、雲去而本覺之月現　塵拂而真如之鏡明

水不波則自定，鑑不翳則自明。故心無可清，去其混之者，而清自現；樂不必尋，去其苦之者，而樂自存。

After clouds have dispersed, the sparkling nature of the moon appears. When the dust is cleaned, the shining truth of the mirror reveals.

Without waves, water is calm. Without dust, the mirror shines. The true nature of human heart is peaceful and happy, so there is no need to find peace and happiness elsewhere. All a person needs to do is to drive away what is dusty and cloudy, and the heart's true nature will appear accordingly.

152、一念能動鬼神　一行克動天地

有一念犯鬼神之禁，一言而傷天地之和，一事而釀子孫之禍者，最宜切戒。

The Supernatural beings can be moved by a trifle idea. The whole universe can be changed by a small act.

Three things people should refrain from doing: any idea that is forbidden by God, any word that will harm universal peace, and any action that will bring disaster to our offspring.

153、情急招損　嚴厲生恨

事有急之不白者，寬之或自明，毋躁急以速其忿；人有操之不從者，縱之或自化，毋操切以益其頑。

Hastiness causes harm. Harshness stirs up hatred.

Time often solves what hastiness fails. Hastiness excites anger. Proper freedom often succeeds where harsh discipline fails. Harshness stirs up rebellious spirit.

154、不能養德　終歸末節

節義傲青雲，文章高白雪，若不以德性陶鎔之，終為血氣之私，技能之末。

Without moral principles, all achievements are but rootless branches.

Lofty conduct and noble writings if not cultivated by moral principles are but impulsive whims skillfully adorned.

155、急流勇退　與世無爭

謝事當謝於正盛之時，居身宜居於獨後之地。

Retreat bravely from the rapid current. Live peacefully with the world.

Leave while the play is good. Stay where there is peace and harmony.

156、慎德於小事　施恩於無緣

謹德須謹於至微之事，施恩務施於不報之人。

Be careful of the trifling matter. Be kind to the total stranger.

Good moral principles should not be neglected even in dealing with a trifling matter. Help should be given to those who cannot possibly repay.

157、文華不如簡素　談今不如述古

交市人不如友山翁，詣朱門不如親白屋；聽街談巷語，不如聞樵歌牧詠；談今人失德過失，不如述古人嘉言懿行。

Simplicity is better than ostentation. Discussing ethical behavior in history is better than gossiping about current events.

Making friends with country folks is better than with city elites. Calling at a common citizen's home is better than visiting a high-ranking official's grand mansion. Listening to the songs of farmers and shepherds is better than to street gossip. Talking about tales of ethical behavior of yesterday is better than discussing the vices of today.

158、修身重德　事業之基

德者事業之基，未有基不固而棟宇堅久者。

A set of moral principles is the cornerstone for any great accomplishment.

A set of moral principles is the cornerstone for any great accomplishment. Without a solid foundation, no building can stand long.

159、心善而子孫盛　根固而枝葉榮

心者後裔之根，未有根不植而枝葉榮茂者。

A kind heart forecasts flourishing offspring. The healthy root produces lush leaves.

Kindness is the root for producing good offspring. It is impossible for a rotten root to produce lush foliage.

160、勿妄自菲薄　勿自誇自傲

前人云：拋卻自家無盡藏，沿門持缽效貧兒。又云：暴富貧兒休說夢，誰家灶裡火無煙。一箴自昧所有，一箴自誇所有，可為學問切戒。

Neither underestimate nor overestimate yourself.

A rich man despite his millions of possessions to live a beggar's life. The penniless child brags about his upstart dream. The former neglects what he actually possesses while the latter gets carried away with what he does not have. Both miss the essence of the golden mean. Same mistakes should be avoided when pursuing knowledge.

161、道乃公正無私　學當隨時警惕

道是一件公眾物事，當隨人而接引；學是一個尋常家飯，當隨時而警惕。

The great way to universal harmony is being just and unselfish. Learning requires constant attention.

The great way to universal harmony is a public avenue, which is accessible to everyone. Learning is daily food, which requires constant attention.

162、信人示己之誠　疑人顯己之詐

信人者，人未必盡誠，己則獨誠矣；疑人者，人未必皆詐，己則先詐矣。

Being trusting shows our honesty. Suspecting signals deceit.

The person who trusts people is trustworthy, though the person whom he trusts may not be. The person who suspects people is deceitful, though the person whom he suspects may not be.

163、春風育物　朔雪殺生

念頭寬厚的，如春風煦育，萬物遭之而生；念頭忌刻的，如朔雪陰凝，萬物遭之而死。

Spring wind brings life to earth. Severe snow puts an end to all life.

A genial person is like the spring wind, which brings life to earth. A mean person is like the severe snow, which puts an end to all life.

164、善根暗長　惡損潛消

為善不見其益，如草裡冬瓜，自應暗長。為惡不見其損，如庭前春雪，當必潛消。

The root of virtue grows in the dark. The damage done by evil will come out sooner or later.

The benefit of virtue is like the wax gourd growing in the grass. Although covered, the fruit will show eventually. The damage done by evil is like the yard covered by the spring snow. Although innocently clean, the real truth will come out sooner or later.

165、厚待故交　禮遇衰朽

遇故舊之交，意氣要愈新；處隱微之事，心跡宜愈顯；待衰朽之
人，恩禮當愈隆。

Be good to old friends. Pay respect to not only the elderly but also the senile.

Show new friendliness to old friends. Be honest in handling secretive matters. Pay deep respect to not only the elderly but also the senile.

166、君子以勤儉立德　小人以勤儉圖利

勤者敏於德義，而世人借勤以濟其貧；儉者淡於貨利，而世人假儉
以飾其吝；君子持身之符，反為小人營私之具矣。惜哉。

A real person is diligent and thrifty to nurture his virtue, while petty people are diligent and thrifty to accumulate personal wealth.

A real person is diligent in performing what is ethical, while petty people are diligent in accumulating personal wealth. A real person is thrifty to free himself from material bondage, while petty people use the name of thrift to cover their stinginess. What the real person uses to cultivate moral character is used by petty people to gain personal profits. What a pity!

167、學貴有恆　道在悟真

憑意興作為者，隨作則隨止，豈是不退之輪；從情識解悟者，有悟則有迷，終非常明之燈。

Great learning depends on perseverance. The essence of Tao is to understand the universal truth.

A person who pursues knowledge on a whim ceases his pursuit when the whim goes off. Knowledge, however, is not a still wheel that will wait for people. A person who sees the light of Tao through emotional perception will feel puzzled again. Without much careful deliberation, the enlightenment is flimsy.

168、律己宜嚴　待人宜寬

人之過誤宜恕，而在己則不可恕；己之困辱宜忍，而在人則不可忍。

Apply strict rules to one's self, but be tolerant to other people.

Forgive other people's faults, but not the faults of our own. Bear our humiliation, but not that of other people's. After all, to be a real person is to provide timely help to those who are in pain.

169、為奇不為異　求清不求激

能脫俗便是奇，作意尚奇者，不為奇而為異；不合汙便是清，絕俗求清者，不為清而為激。

Be unique but not weird. Be clean but not extreme.

Being unique is not to be confined by what is conventional. It is not unique but weird for a person to go out of his way to be unconventional. Being clean is to reject what is foul and evil. It is not clean but extreme for a person to cut off all socially accepted behavior.

170、恩宜自薄而厚　威須先嚴後寬

恩宜自淡而濃，先濃後淡者，人忘其惠；威宜自嚴而寬，先寬後嚴者，人怨其酷。

Increase favors progressively. Relax discipline gradually.

Increase favors progressively lest people not appreciate your kindness. Decrease discipline gradually lest people complain about your severity.

171、心虛意淨　明心見性

心虛則性現，不息心而求見性，如撥波覓月。意淨則心清，不了意而求明心，如索鏡增塵。

Drive away intruders from the heart to recover its genuine state.

Undue desires are intruders of the heart. The true nature of the heart is peaceful and happy. Without undue desires, the heart's true nature appears. Trying to find the heart's true nature when it is loaded with undue desires is as impossible as to catch a peaceful moon in high waves. Without anxiety, the heart is peaceful. Trying to find a peaceful heart when it is full of anxiety is as impossible as to find a clean mirror in piles of dust.

172、人情冷暖　世態炎涼

我貴而人奉之，奉此峨冠大帶也；我賤而人侮之，侮此布衣草履也。然則原非奉我，我胡為喜，原非侮我，我胡為怒。

People's attitude changes in accordance with our social status in the world.

When I am high up in an important post, people flatter me. What they flatter is the high important post. When I am down in a low humble position, people despise me. What they despise is the low humble position. They neither flatter nor despise the actual me. Why should I feel joyful or angry at their different attitudes.

173、慈悲之心　生生之機

為鼠常留飯，憐蛾不點燈，古人此等念頭，是吾人一點生生之機。無此，便所謂土木形骸而已。

Kindness kindles the light for life.

People in old days used to leave rice for mice and put out light to spare the moth. Their motive is to save lives. Without this bit of kindness, we are no difference from the figures made of wood and clay.

174、勿為欲情所繫　便與本體相合

心體便是天體。一念之喜，景星慶雲；一念之怒，震雷暴雨；一念之慈，和風甘露；一念之嚴，烈日秋霜。何者少得。只要隨起隨滅，廓然無礙，便與太虛同體。

When a person is not dominated by emotions, he and the universe merge into one.

We are the universe. Happiness brings shining stars and rosy clouds. Anger causes frightening thunderstorms. Tenderness calls in the gentle breezes and silky dews. Harshness produces the scorching sun and biting frost. None of the natural phenomena is missing in the human heart. If we can follow the example of the universe and let emotions come and go accordingly without being controlled by them, we and the universe merge into one.

175、無事寂寂以照惺惺　有事惺惺以主寂寂

無事時，心易昏冥，宜寂寂而照以惺惺。有事時，心易奔逸，宜惺惺而主以寂寂。

In comfort, be alert. In turmoil, be calm.

People should keep alert while in comfort, for that is the time easily for them to be muddleheaded. People should stay calm while in turmoil, for that is the time easily for them to feel panic.

176、明利害之情　忘利害之慮

議事者，身在事外，宜悉利害之情。任事者，身居事中，當忘利害之慮。

Understand the pros and cons of an event. Worry about neither gains nor losses.

An arbitrator should not get involved in an event in order to make a fair judgment. The performer should devote himself whole-heartedly to whatever he is working on without worrying about personal gains or losses.

177、操持嚴明　守正不阿

　　士君子處權門要路，操履要嚴明，心氣要和易，毋少隨腥羶之黨，亦毋過激而犯蜂蠆之毒。

Be honest and fair without yielding to pressures.

　　When a real person is trusted with power, he should be honest and fair in behavior but peaceful in attitude. He should neither associate with evil parties, nor go overboard to provoke malicious attacks.

178、渾然和氣　處世珍寶

　　標節義者，必以節義受謗；榜道學者，常因道學招尤；故君子不近惡事，亦不立善名，只渾然和氣，才是居身之珍。

Geniality is the golden rule of conduct.

　　When a person is proud of his ethical behavior, his ethical behavior becomes the cause for slander. When a person boasts of his great learning, his great learning becomes the target for criticism. That is why a real person keeps away from vice but claims nothing virtuous. Geniality is the golden rule for him to conduct himself in the world.

179、誠心和氣陶冶暴惡　名義氣節激勵邪曲

遇欺詐之人，以誠心感動之；遇暴戾之人，以和氣薰蒸之；遇邪惡私曲之人，以名義氣節激礪之；天下無不入我陶冶中矣。

Sincerity and geniality move the violent and the vicious. Honor and integrity rehabilitate the crooked.

Move the deceitful with sincerity, influence the violent with geniality, and encourage the crooked with honor and integrity so that no one will be left uncultivated.

180、和氣致祥瑞　潔白留清名

一念慈祥，可以醞釀兩間和氣；寸心潔白，可以昭垂百代清芬。

Geniality brings good fortune. Purity results in a good reputation.

A kind thought brings peace. A heart without evil desires results in a good reputation for generations.

181、庸德庸行　和平之基

　　陰謀怪習，異行奇能，俱是涉世的禍胎。只一個庸德庸行，便可以完混沌而召和平。

Moderation is the foundation for everlasting peace.

Crafty tricks, peculiar habits, eccentric behavior, and strange feats all lead to disaster. Moderation is the foundation for everlasting peace.

182、忍得住耐得過　則得自在之境

　　語云：登山耐險路，踏雪耐危橋。一耐字極有意味。如傾險之人情，坎坷之世道，若不得一耐字撐過去，幾何不墮入榛莽坑塹哉。

One who understands the essence of tolerance enjoys peace and comfort everywhere.

An old Chinese saying tells us that climbing mountains one should tolerate the dangerous trail, and walking in the snow one should tolerate the unsafe broken wooden bridge. The key word "tolerance" is worth pondering over. In this world, human relations are unstable, and life is hard. If a person doesn't know how to tolerate, it is difficult for him not to fall into the abyss of great sadness and distress.

183、心體瑩然　不失本真

誇逞功業，炫耀文章，皆是靠外物做人。不知心體瑩然，本來不失，即無寸功隻字，亦自有堂堂正正做人處。

Keep the heart free from contamination. Keep the heart in its original state.

To boast of accomplishments is to borrow outside factors to reinforce a person's real value. A person who accomplishes nothing great but keeps his heart in its original state free from contamination is worthy of praise.

184、忙裡偷閒　鬧中取靜

忙裡要偷閑，須先向閑時討個欛柄；鬧中要取靜，須先從靜處立個主宰。不然，未有不因境而遷，隨時而靡者。

Find time to relax when pressed by a heavy schedule. Stay calm in turmoil.

Finding time to relax when pressed by a busy schedule, one has to make preparations when not heavily occupied. To stay calm in turmoil, one should learn self-discipline when all is peaceful and well. Anyone who fails to do so will certainly be overpowered by circumstances.

185、為天地立心　為生民立命　為子孫造福

不昧己心，不拂人情，不竭物力。三者可以為天地立心，為生民立命，為子孫造福。

Set a good example in the universe. Work for the benefit of human beings. Create prosperity for offspring.

If a person does not suppress his conscience, oppose humanity, or waste natural resources, he is able to set good examples in the universe, to work for the benefit of human race, and to create prosperity for our offspring.

186、為官公廉　居家恕儉

居官有二語，曰唯公則生明，唯廉則生威。居家有二語，曰唯恕則情平，唯儉則用足。

Be fair and honest to be a government official. Be forgiving and thrifty to build a family

It is important for a government official to be fair and honest. Fairness leads to a correct and brilliant judgment; honesty wins people's respect. It is important to be forgiving and thrifty to build a family. Forgiveness brings peace, and thrift prevents inadequacy.

187、處富知貧　居安思危

處富貴之地，要知貧賤的痛癢；當少壯之時，須念衰老的辛酸。

The wealthy should know what poverty is like. When in safety one should make preparations for danger.

When wealthy and powerful, one should know the hardship of the poor. When young and strong, one should understand the misery of the old.

188、清濁並包　善惡相容

持身不可太皎潔，一切汙辱垢穢，要茹納得；與人不可太分明，一切善惡賢愚，要包容得。

Accept both the clean and the dirty. Take both the good and the bad.

It is not proper to place undue emphasis on being clean. To be able to tolerate the dirty is important. It is not proper to draw a distinctive line between the good and the bad. To accept all kinds of people without discrimination is recommended.

189、勿仇小人　勿媚君子

休與小人仇讎，小人自有對頭；休向君子諂媚，君子原無私惠。

Don't be an enemy to the petty. Don't flatter the virtuous.

Don't be an enemy to the petty, as there will be their rivals to deal with them. Don't flatter the virtuous, for the virtuous don't grant personal favors.

190、疾病易醫　魔障難除

縱欲之病可醫，而執理之病難醫；事物之障可除，而義理之障難除。

To cure the physical disease is easy. To expel irrationality is difficult.

Overindulging in undue desires is possible to be curbed, but rectifying an irrational conviction is difficult. Removing a material obstacle is possible, but correcting a misinterpreted ethical concept is difficult.

191、金須百煉　矢不輕發

磨礪當如百煉之金，急就者非邃養；施為似千鈞之弩，輕發者，無宏功。

Gold requires numerous refinements. To shoot an arrow needs sound preparation.

Good character is like gold which requires numerous refinements. Anything hastily accomplished is easily outshone. Without sound preparation, neither a great talent nor an excellent giant bow will achieve high. What recklessly performed will be easily outdone.

192、寧為小人所毀　勿為君子所容

寧為小人所忌毀，毋為小人所媚悅；寧為君子所責備，毋為君子所包容。

Rather defamed by the petty than tolerated by the virtuous.

It is better to be defamed than praised by the petty. It is better to be criticized than tolerated by the virtuous.

193、好利者害顯而淺　好名者害隱而深

好利者，逸出於道義之外，其害顯而淺；好名者，竄入於道義之中，其害隱而深。

Damage caused by the profit chaser is obvious but small. Damage caused by the fame seeker is covered but serious.

Profit chasers renounce moral principles openly; therefore, the damage they cause is obvious but small. Fame seekers are disguised as virtuous ; therefore, the damage they cause is covered but serious.

194、忘恩報怨　刻薄之尤

受人之恩，雖深不報，怨則淺亦報之；聞人之惡，雖隱不疑，善則顯亦疑之。此刻之極，薄之尤也，宜切戒之。

Ingratitude and retaliation are most spiteful.

To forget big favors but to retaliate against trifling offences is most spiteful, so is to believe the clearly groundless slander but to doubt the most manifest virtue. Be sure to commit neither of them.

195、讒言如雲蔽日　甘言如風侵肌

讒夫毀士，如寸雲蔽日，不久自明；媚子阿人，似隙風侵肌，不覺其損。

Slander is like the dark cloud to the sun. Flattery is like the cool comfortable draft.

A real person who suffers malicious slander is like the sun overshadowed by the cloud; his true nature will appear before long. Flattery is like the cool and comfortable draft; its harm is certain but not to be felt at once.

196、戒高絕之行　忌褊急之衷

山之高峻處無木，而谿谷迴環，則草木叢生；水之湍急處無魚，而淵潭停蓄，則魚鱉聚集。此高絕之行，褊急之衷，君子重有戒焉。

Restrain from proud and extreme behavior. Avoid making biased and hasty decisions.

Few trees grow on the high mountaintop, but plenty can be found in the lower valley. Few fish can be found in rapid currents, but many in peaceful deeper waters. A real person should avoid being proud, extreme, biased, and hasty.

197、虛圓立業　僨事失機

建功立業者，多虛圓之士；僨事失機者，必執拗之人。

Be flexible and modest to win success. Inflexibility leads to failure.

Modest and flexible people are able to win great victory. Those who are stubborn and headstrong often miss the golden chance to be successful.

198、處世要道　不即不離

處世不宜與俗同，亦不宜與俗異。做事不宜令人厭，亦不宜令人喜。

The golden rule of conduct is to observe the golden mean.

To be neither exactly the same with nor completely different from the conventional is the golden rule of conduct in life. To neither please nor annoy people on purpose is the golden rule of doing a job.

199、老當益壯　大器晚成

日既暮而猶煙霞絢爛，歲將晚而更橙橘芳馨；故末路晚年，君子更宜精神百倍。

The older a person grows, the stronger he should be. Great vessels completed late.

At sunset, the rosy clouds are magnificent. At the end of the year, oranges yield pleasant fragrance. A real person in his old age should live with even greater zest to accomplish even greater achievements.

200、藏才隱智　任重致遠

鷹立如睡，虎行似病，正是牠攫鳥噬人手段。故君子要聰明不露，才華不逞，才有肩鴻任鉅的力量。

Conceal talent and wisdom to take on greater and more difficult responsibilities.

The standing eagle looks as if asleep, and the walking tiger's steps suggest illness. Both are disguises to catch their prey. Similarly, a real person should reveal neither his wisdom nor his ability in order to shoulder greater and more difficult responsibilities.

201、過儉者吝嗇　過讓者卑曲

儉，美德也，過則為慳吝，為鄙嗇，反傷雅道；讓，懿行也，過則為足恭，為曲謹，多出機心。

Excessive thrift is stingy. Excessive modesty is flattering.

Thrift is a great virtue. Excessive thrift is stinginess, which is against the rule of good conduct. Modesty is praiseworthy. Excessive modesty is flattering, which often shelters trickery.

202、喜憂安危　勿介於心

毋憂拂意，毋喜快心，毋恃久安，毋憚初難。

Don't cling to feelings of happiness, anxiety, security, or danger.

Don't worry about adversity. Don't rejoice in good fortune. Don't depend on lasting security. Don't be afraid of the difficulty at the beginning.

203、宴樂、聲色、名位，三者不可過貪

宴飲之樂多，不是個好人家；聲華之習勝，不是個好士子；名位之念重，不是個好臣士。

Don't overindulge in pursuing parties, sensual pleasures, or high positions.

A good family does not give many parties, a good scholar does not value sensual pleasures, and a good government official does not regard high position or fame as an important matter.

204、樂極生悲　苦盡甘來

世人以心愜處為樂，卻被樂心引入苦處；達士以心拂處為樂，終為苦心換得樂來。

Happiness at its height gives rise to sorrow. The end of bitter hardship comes sweet happiness.

Common people often feel happy when their undue desires are fulfilled, but they don't know fulfilled desires often give rise to sorrow. Enlightened people find happiness in adversity. They know real joy comes only after difficulties are overcome.

205、遇滿則溢　過剛則折

居盈滿者，如水之將溢未溢，切忌再加一滴；處危急者，如木之將折未折，切忌再加一搦。

It is easy to overflow when full. It is easy to break when rigid.

A person at the peak of his success is like a container filled to its brim. Don't add even one more drop, or it will overflow. The person in a dangerous situation is like a dry and rigid twig at its breaking point. Don't give even a slightest pressure, or it will snap.

206、冷靜觀人　理智處世

冷眼觀人，冷耳聽語，冷情當感，冷心思理。

Observe objectively and conduct life rationally.

Observe objectively with objective ears and eyes. Conduct life rationally with a clear head.

207、量寬福厚　器小祿薄

　　仁人心地寬舒，便福厚而慶長，事事成個寬舒氣象；鄙夫念頭迫促，便祿薄而澤短，事事得個迫促規模。

A generous person enjoys abundant blessings. A mean person scanty.

A person's fortune is in proportion to his generosity and capacity for tolerance. A kind and generous person is blessed with abundant and long-lasting good fortune, and his life is joyful and prosperous. A mean and stingy person enjoys only meager and short-lived one, and his life is marked with perpetual worries and inadequacy.

208、惡不可即就　善不可急親

　　聞惡不可就惡，恐為讒夫洩怒；聞善不可即親，恐引奸人進身。

Both vice and virtue need close inspection.

Don't show immediate resentment upon hearing of a person's vice, which may be only a malicious rumor plotted by evil people to harm him; or show approval hastily upon hearing of a virtue, which may only be a maneuver used by the evil to gain their personal interests.

209、燥性僨事　和平徼福

性燥心粗者，一事無成；心和氣平者，百福自集。

Imprudence ruins success. Peace invites good fortune.

Anyone who is impatient and imprudent will accomplish nothing. A peaceful person always attracts good fortune.

210、酷則失善人，濫則招惡友

用人不宜刻，刻則思效者去。交友不宜濫，濫則貢諛者來。

Excessive demands drive the loyal away. Being without principles draws flatterers.

It is not proper to be overly demanding towards those who are at your service. Excessive demands drive the loyal away. It is proper to have principles in choosing friends, or flatterers come.

211、急處站得穩　高處看得準　危險徑地早回頭

風斜雲急處，要立得腳定；花濃柳豔處，要著得眼高；路危徑險處，要回得頭早。

Stand firmly to face the challenge. See clearly when high up on the top. Be willing to turn back immediately on a dangerous road.

Stand firmly in the storm. Set lofty principles when in good fortune. Turn back early on a dangerous road.

212、和衷以濟節義　謙德以承功名

節義之人濟以和衷，才不啟忿爭之路；功名之士承以謙德，方不開嫉妒之門。

Temper upright character with gentleness. Sustain great success with modesty.

Upright character tempered with tenderness closes the road to conflict. Great success sustained with modesty shuts the door on jealousy.

213、居官有節度　鄉居敦舊交

士大夫居官，不可竿牘無節，要使人難見，以杜倖端；居鄉不可崖岸太高，要使人易見，以敦舊好。

A government official should observe the rule of propriety. A retired public servant should be friendly to old acquaintances.

A government official should observe the rule of propriety. He should make it difficult for people to reach him so as to prevent flattery and dishonorable attempts to win his favors. Having relieved of official duties, the retired public servant should make it easy for old acquaintances to reach him so as to renew friendships.

214、事上敬謹　待下寬仁

大人不可不畏，畏大人則無放逸之心；小民亦不可不畏，畏小民則無豪橫之名。

Be respectful to the superior. Be kind to the subordinate.

Both the superior and the subordinate should be treated with great care. Being respectful to the superior will check negligence. Being kind to the subordinate prevents from obtaining the name of bully.

215、處逆境時比於下　心怠荒時思於上

事稍拂逆，便思不如我的人，則怨尤自消；心稍怠荒，便思勝似我的人，則精神自奮。

Think of our inferiors when the fortune is against us. Think of our superiors when indulging in comforts.

Thinking of our inferiors when the fortune is against us stops all complaints naturally. Thinking of our superiors when we are indulging in comforts spurs us on at once.

216、不輕諾，不生嗔，不多事，不倦怠

不可乘喜而輕諾，不可因醉而生嗔，不可乘快而多事，不可困倦而鮮終。

Don't give imprudent promises. Don't lose temper. Don't be elaborate. Don't be careless.

Don't give imprudent promises when happy. Don't use bad temper to cover a shame. Don't be elaborate when things go well. Don't be careless because of fatigue.

217、讀書讀到樂處　觀物觀入化境

善讀書者，要讀到手舞足蹈處，方不落筌蹄；善觀物者，要觀到心融神洽時，方不泥跡象。

Understand the essential message of a book.
Recognize the soul of an object.

A good reader will not confine himself to the written words. Instead, he recognizes the implicit message the author wishes to impart. A good observer does not restrict himself to the superficial appearance of an object. Instead, he penetrates its innermost soul.

218、勿逞所長以形人之短　勿恃所有以凌人之貧

天賢一人，以誨眾人之愚，而世反逞所長，以形人之短；天富一人，以濟眾人之困，而世反挾所有，以凌人之貧。真天之戮民哉。

Don't display strength to expose other people's weakness. Don't use wealth to exploit those in poverty.

Heaven grants ability to a selected few to assist the common majority. With the gift from Heaven those selected few humiliate them instead. Heaven trusts wealth to a selected few to help the needy mass. With the gift from Heaven those selected few exploit them instead. Heaven truly condemns those few.

219、上智下愚可與論學　中才之人難與下手

　　至人何思何慮，愚人不識不知，可與論學亦可與建功；唯中才的人，多一番思慮知識，便多一番臆度猜疑，事事難與下手。

It is possible to discuss great knowledge with the most and the least intelligent. It is hard to enlighten the mediocre.

The most intelligent are open-minded, and the least intelligent are innocent. They are the people with whom it is possible to discuss great knowledge and accomplish something important. As for the mediocre, they are the people difficult to work with because knowledge and intelligence to them are but sources for anxiety and suspicion.

220、守口須密　防意須嚴

　　口乃心之門，守口不密，洩盡真機；意乃心之足，防意不嚴，走盡邪蹊。

Shut the mouth tightly. Check the intention seriously.

The mouth is the door of the heart. The person who cannot keep his mouth tightly shut lets out secrets without reservation. Intention is the feet of the heart. The person who cannot check his intention seriously cannot prevent himself from traveling to the land of evil.

221、責人宜寬　責己宜苛

責人者，原無過於有過之中，則情平；責己者，求有過於無過之內，則德進。

Be kind when criticizing people. Be severe when criticizing oneself.

When criticize people, try to find forgivable reasons for their mistakes; thus the flame of our anger will be quenched. When criticize oneself, try to find fault within what seems perfect; thus our own moral character will be cultivated.

222、幼不學　不成器

子弟者，大人之胚胎；秀才者，士大夫之胚胎。此時若火力不到，陶鑄不純，他日涉世立朝，終難成個令器。

Anyone who fails to study when young will be of little value when grown up.

Children are embryonic adults. Young scholars are embryonic government officials. If these embryos are not nurtured and trained properly now, they will be of little value tomorrow.

223、不憂患難　不畏權豪

君子處患難而不憂，當宴遊而惕慮，遇豪權而不懼，對惸獨而驚心。

Don't worry about adversity. Don't be afraid of the wealthy or powerful.

A real person does not worry in times of adversity but keeps alert during times of merriment. He is not afraid of the wealthy or the powerful but is greatly concerned about the lonely, the elderly, and the orphaned.

224、濃夭淡久　大器晚成

桃李雖豔，何如松蒼柏翠之堅貞；梨杏雖甘，何如橙黃橘綠之馨冽。信乎，濃夭不及淡久，早秀不如晚成也。

The lavish soon disappear while the plain persist. Things of great value take a long time to develop.

Magnificent plum and pear blossoms wither soon while the plain cedars and pines persist. The fragrance of sweet pears and apricots are less stimulating than that of oranges and tangerines. It is true that the plain outlives the lavish, and the late success is of greater value than the early one.

225、靜中見真境　淡中識本然

風恬浪靜中，見人生之真境；味淡聲稀處，識心體之本然。

Life's true state exists in tranquility. Heart's true nature appears when undue desires are gone.

Life's true state is found in peace and tranquility. Heart's true nature appears when it is free from undue desires.

226、言者多不顧行　論者未必真知

談山林之樂者，未必真得山林之趣；厭名利之談者，未必盡忘名利之情。

A person may not practice what he advocates. People may not truly reject what they disgust.

The person who advocates country living may not truly enjoy what he advocates. Those who think wealth and power are disgusting may not truly reject them.

227、無為無作　優遊清逸

釣水，逸事也，尚持生殺之柄；奕棋，清戲也，且動戰爭之心。可見喜事不如省事之為適；多能不若無能之全真。

Live a leisure life with neither special purposes nor efforts.

Fishing is a peaceful pastime, yet it involves life and death. Playing chess is a friendly game, yet it ignites the war spirit. It is true that a leisure life without any specific purposes is more enjoyable than a heavily engaged one, and that without special talents is closer to genuine human nature than to be versatile.

228、春色為人間之妝飾　秋氣見天地之真吾

鶯花茂而山濃谷豔，總是乾坤之幻境；水木落而石瘦崖枯，才見天地之真吾。

Spring decorates the earth. Fall exposes its true nature.

Lush green mountains and valleys decorated with colorful flowers and sweet bird songs are but illusions of the universe. The true state of the earth is the rock revealed after the stream has dried, and the cliff exposed after trees have shed all their leaves.

229、世間之廣狹　皆由於自造

歲月本長，而忙者自促；天地本寬，而鄙者自隘；風花雪月本閒，而勞攘者自冗。

The size of the universe depends on the individual.

Time is long; for the person with a heavy schedule it is short. The world is vast; for the narrow-minded it is tight. Spring flowers, summer breezes, the fall moon, and the winter snow are but natural phenomena, but the fussy person troubles himself with superfluous sentiments.

230、樂貴自然真趣　量物不在多遠

得趣不在多，盆池拳石間，煙霞俱足；會心不在遠，蓬窗竹屋下，風月自賒。

Most enjoyable elements exist in what is most simple and natural. True value does not depend on quantity or distance.

The enjoyable elements do not necessarily exist in something grand. The delightful morning mist and colorful evening clouds can be found over a fist-sized rock in a basin-sized pond. Pleasant features can be found not necessarily somewhere far away. The bright moon and gentle breezes liger about the thatched window of the bamboo hut.

231、心靜而本體現　水清而月影明

聽靜夜之鐘聲，喚醒夢中之夢；觀澄潭之月影，窺見身外之身。

When the heart is in the state of tranquility, its true nature appears. When the water is clean, the reflection of the moon is clear.

Life is but a dream. In a quiet night, the tolling bell awakens a dream within the dream. The roles people play in the world are but illusive. In a clean pond, the reflection of the moon reveals the role above this one.

232、天地萬物　皆是實相

鳥語蟲聲，總是傳心之訣；花英草色，無非見道之文。學者要天機清澈，胸次玲瓏，觸物皆有會心處。

Everything in the universe conveys heavenly truth.

Heaven speaks through nature. Birds, insects, flowers, and grasses are all his messengers. If a person will clear away the obstacles in his heart, heavenly messages can be found everywhere.

233、觀形不如觀心　神用勝過跡用

人解讀有字書，不解讀無字書；知彈有弦琴，不知彈無弦琴。以跡用，不以神用，何以得琴書之趣。

Observing a person's heart is more important than his physical appearance. A person's soul can achieve what the physical body fails.

People understand the contents of a book through written words. Without words, they are lost. People make music by playing on the strings of a stringed instrument. Without the strings, they are helpless. In life, many interesting things are written not in words, and a great deal of delightful sound is produced not on strings. Knowing only the tangible body not the intangible soul is hard to truly enjoy the fun of books and music.

234、心無物欲乾坤靜　坐有琴書便是仙

心無物欲，即是秋空霽海；坐有琴書，便成石室丹丘。

The world is peaceful when the heart is void of undue desires. Accompanied by books and music, every person can be a carefree deity.

When a person is free from undue desires, his heart is like the clear autumn sky without any clouds or the peaceful ocean after the raging storm. When he is accompanied by books and music, he feels as happy as a carefree celestial being.

235、歡樂極兮哀情多　興味濃後感索然

賓朋雲集，劇飲淋漓樂矣。俄而漏盡燭殘，香銷茗冷，不覺反成嘔咽，令人索然無味。天下事率類此，奈何不早回頭也。

Happiness at its height turns into sorrow. Excessive savor becomes flat.

One of the happiest things in life is to drink merrily with a lot of friends. However, when the night has run its course, the candles burn down, the tea is cold, and the aroma of food and wine die away; the party is over. Then, happiness is changed to desolation, laughter tears, and the sick feeling of nausea replaces the great feeling of joy. Nothing under the sun is an exception to this pattern. Why not turn back early?

236、知機真神乎　會趣明道矣

會得個中趣，五湖之煙月盡入寸裡；破得眼前機，千古之英雄盡歸掌握。

Know the fundamental principle of the universe. Appreciate the unique beauty of the world.

Any person who has the ability to appreciate the unique beauty of the common object gets the secret of the beauty in the universe. Any person who understands the basic principle of daily life grasps the essence of the true heroes of yesterday and today.

237、萬象皆空幻　達人須達觀

　　山河大地已屬微塵，而況塵中之塵；血肉身軀且歸泡影，而況影外之影。非上上智，無了了心。

Everything in this universe is but an illusion. An enlightened person should free himself from worldly bondage.

High mountains and great rivers are but tiny specks in comparison with the boundless universe, not to mention that teeny tiny speck of those specks, the human body. The physical body lasts as short as the shadow of a soap bubble, not to mention the shadow of that shadow, the worldly fame and wealth. It takes great wisdom to recognize illusions and to be freed from worldly bondage.

238、泡沫人生　何爭名利

　　石火光中爭長競短，幾何光陰；蝸牛角上較雌論雄，許大世界。

Life is but an empty soap bubble. Why compete for fame and wealth?

Is it worth competing for power and wealth in a life as short as the flint spark? Even if you win, how long can it last? Is it wise to fight for worldly gains in a world as small as the snail's horn? Even if you are the winner, how big a place does it belong to you?

239、極端空寂　過猶不及

　　寒燈無焰，敝裘無溫，總是播弄光景；身如槁木，心似死灰，不免墮在頑空。

To reject materialism totally is as bad as to accept it wholeheartedly.

It is lamentable when the lamp is cold without fire, and the threadbare fur coat fails to keep warm. Life will be meaningless when a person treats his body as the dried-out wood and his heart as the cold ash. Rejecting materialism totally is as bad as to accept it wholeheartedly.

240、得好休時便好休　如不休時終無休

　　人肯當下休，便當下了。若要尋個歇處，則婚嫁雖完，事亦不少。僧道雖好，心亦不了。前人云：「如今休去，便休去，若覓了時，無了時。」見之卓矣。

Put burden down now, or you will never be able to do so in the future.

A person's burden leaves him as soon as he puts it down. Don't wish to wait for a proper moment to do so, for the moment will never come. Since marriage is generally considered the most important thing in life, many people feel that after marriage there should be nothing left to be worried about. As a matter of fact, marriage only introduces more worries. A monk's life is commonly believed simple and trouble-free. In fact, a monk is never carefree. An old Chinese saying points it out wisely, "Put burden down now. Don't wait for a proper moment which will never come."

241、冷靜觀世事　忙中去偷閒

從冷視熱，然後知熱處之奔馳無益；從冗入閒，然後覺閒中之滋味最長。

Observe the world objectively. Take time out from the busy schedule to relax.

Only a calm and objective observer will truly realize how futile it is to compete eagerly for power and wealth. Only the person who has experienced the heavy pressure of work will truly appreciate the value of leisure time.

242、不觀富貴　不溺酒色

有浮雲富貴之風，而不必岩棲穴處；無膏肓泉石之癖，而常自醉酒耽詩。

Don't be seduced by wealth or power. Don't indulge in sensual activities.

He who views wealth and power as floating clouds does not have to live in a remote area. Although mountains and waters may provide great pleasure to an enlightened person, poetry and wine will do him just the same.

243、恬淡適己　身心自在

競逐聽人，而不嫌盡醉。恬淡適己，而不誇獨醒。此釋氏所謂不為法纏，不為空纏。

How much one should value worldly gains depends on the individual. To feel totally at ease with yourself is what it counts.

Don't criticize those who are devoted to worldly gains or speak of yourself in superlatives. Buddha teaches us to insist upon neither material profits nor spiritual emptiness. To feel totally at ease with yourself is what it counts.

244、廣狹長短　由於心念

延促由於一念，寬窄繫之寸心。故機閒者，一日遙於千古；意廣者，斗室寬若兩間。

The human mind determines the size of the world.

The human mind determines the size of the world. To those who do not waste time on cunning maneuvers, one day is longer than a thousand years. To a person with great tolerance, a small room is as big as two.

245、栽花種竹　心境無我

損之又損，栽花種竹，儘交還烏有先生。忘無可忘，焚香煮茗，總不問白衣童子。

Even in leisure activities, one keeps being selfless.

Cut, cut, cut. Cut down the sense of self- esteem to the minimum even when gardening. Forget, forget, forget. Forget the world around totally even when burning incense sticks and cooking tea.

246、知足則仙凡路異　善用則生殺自殊

都來眼前事，知足者仙境，不知足者凡境；總出世上因，善用者生機，不善用者殺機。

Contentment differentiates the common from the divine. Life or death depends on the individual.

There is only one world. To the content, it is a paradise□but to the discontent, it is a place of distress. The world is built on cause and consequence. Those who plant life will reap life and plant death will get death.

247、守正安分　遠禍之道

趨炎附勢之禍，甚慘亦甚速；棲恬守逸之味，最淡亦最長。

Following what is righteous and being content with what we have are best ways to ward off disaster.

The downfall of those who flatter the powerful and wealthy is cruel and imminent. The happiness of those who are content with a quiet and peaceful life is plain but long-lasting.

248、與閒雲為友　以風月為家

松澗邊，攜杖獨行，立處雲生破衲；竹窗下，枕書高臥，覺時月浸寒氈。

Make friends with idle clouds. Feel at home with the wind and the moon.

What a pleasant time it is for a person with only a staff in hand to walk alone by a stream in the pine forest, and when he comes to a halt□the mountain mist has crept into his old worn-out overalls. What a delightful experience it is for him to rest his head on a pile of books to sleep under the bamboo window, and when he wakes, the moon light has penetrated his thin blanket.

249、存道心　消幻業

色慾火熾，而一念及病時，便興似寒灰；名利飴甘，而一想到死地，便味如嚼蠟。故人常憂死慮病，亦可消幻業而長道心。

Bear the principle of right conduct in mind to stop deceptive illusions.

When a person is hot with sensual desires, the thought of disease will turn the desires into cold ashes. When a person is indulged in the sweetness of power and wealth, the thought of death will take away its juicy flavor. Thoughts of disease and death help stop deceptive illusions and inspire people to pursue the real truth of life.

250、退步寬平　清淡悠久

爭先的徑路窄，退後一步，自寬平一步。濃豔的滋味短，清淡一分，自悠長一分。

Compromise makes a road broad and smooth. Strong passions shorten the period of enjoyment.

The road of competition is narrow. To yield a step is to gain a step in broadness. Strong passions do not endure long. To cut down an inch on passions is to gain an inch on the length of enjoyment.

251、修養定靜工夫　臨變方不動亂

忙處不亂性，須閒處心神養得清。死時不動心，須生時事物看得破。

Stay composed to prevent acting foolishly at the crucial moment.

A composed attitude in turmoil depends on the self-discipline cultivated in peacetime. The tranquility felt at the death bed results from the profound insight of life formed while alive.

252、隱者無榮辱　道義無炎涼

隱逸林中無榮辱，道義路上無炎涼。

Humiliation or glory is strange to those who are indifferent to wealth or power. Snobbery does not exist among those who value only ethics.

Humiliation or glory is strange to those who are indifferent to worldly power or wealth. Snobbery does not exist among those who value only ethics.

253、去思苦亦樂　隨心熱亦涼

　　熱不必除，而除此熱惱，身常在清涼臺上；窮不可遣，而遣此窮愁，心常居安樂窩中。

Happiness arrives when anguish is removed. Comfort arrives when anxiety is driven away.

There is no need to remove heat. Stop worrying about heat, coolness arrives at once. Poverty cannot be driven away. Stop worrying about poverty, peace and happiness appears instantly.

254、居安思危　處進思退

　　進步處便思退步，庶免觸藩之禍；著手時先圖放手，才脫騎虎之危。

Prepare for possible dangers while yet safe; plan for a likely departure in the beginning.

To plan for all likely dangers in advance precludes a disastrous ruin. To prepare for departure in the beginning excludes the danger of an awkward stalemate.

255、貪得者雖富亦貧　知足者雖貧亦富

　　貪得者，分金恨不得玉，封公怨不授侯，權豪自甘乞丐；知足者，藜羹旨於膏粱，布袍煖於狐貉，編民不讓王公。

The greedy though rich are but poor. The contented though poor are yet rich.

A greedy person always feels sorry. When he has gold, he feels sorry for not getting jade. When he is granted the rank of count, he feels sorry for not being given the position of king. With all the power and wealth in his hand, he behaves like a beggar. To a contented person, weeds taste better than meat, and the cotton robe keeps the body warmer than the fur. Common as he is, the contented person is much nobler than the one with a glamorous title.

256、隱者高明　省事平安

　　矜名不若逃名趣，練事何如省事閒。

Those who hunt for neither power nor wealth are wise. Those who save trouble enjoy peace.

The fame escaper is wiser than the fame hunter. Those who simplify things to save trouble will enjoy more leisure time than those who run into great trouble for making things elaborate.

257、超越喧寂　悠然自適

嗜寂者，觀白雲幽石而通玄；趨榮者，見清歌妙舞而忘倦。唯自得之士，無喧寂，無榮枯，無往非自適之天。

To be influenced by neither silence nor noise. Feel at ease with the world as it is.

A quiet person finds inspiration in clouds and rocks. A merry-loving person forgets fatigue in songs and dances. Only the enlightened one influenced by neither silence nor noise is at ease with the world as it is.

258、得道無牽繫　靜燥兩無關

孤雲出岫，去留一無所繫；朗鏡懸空，靜躁兩不相干。

After enlightenment, a person stays undisturbed by either silence or noise.

An enlightened person, free as the lonely cloud over the mountain top, is traceless. An enlightened person, bright as the luminous moon high up in the sky, is beyond the influence of the world around.

259、濃處味短　淡中趣長

　　悠長之趣，不得於醲釅，而得於啜菽飲水之餘；惆恨之懷，不生於枯寂，而生於品竹調絲之後。固知濃處味常短，淡中趣獨真也。

Rich flavor does not last. Simple taste endures.

　　People are easier to be sated with high quality wine than simple water and bean porridge, and to feel sorry after merry parties than during quiet days. This is the best proof that the elaborate and rich do not last, but the simple and common endure.

260、理出於易　道不在遠

　　禪宗曰：飢來吃飯倦來眠。詩旨曰：眼前景致口頭語。蓋極高寓於極平，至難出於至易，有意者反遠，無心者自近也。

Great philosophies are conceived in simple matters. Tao is close at hand.

　　Zen Buddhism teaches us to eat when hungry and to sleep when tired. The principle of poetry writing tells us to use ordinary daily language to describe what is common at hand. Just as great oaks from little acorns grow, the supreme always rises from the base, and the most difficult comes from the easiest. This also explains why a person of fixed purpose often achieves the opposite of what he wishes, but the one without particular desires will be rewarded the best for him.

261、動靜合宜　出入無礙

水流而石無聲，得處喧見寂之趣；山高而雲不礙，悟出有入無之機。

No obstacle will hinder his progress when a person acts properly to the situation.

The rock in the river is not disturbed even though the water gurgles. This tells that to stay calm in turmoil is admirable. High mountains can never impede floating clouds. This reveals that to discard strong desires is to gain complete freedom.

262、執著是苦海　解脫是仙鄉

山林是勝地，一營戀便成市朝；書畫是雅事，一貪癡便成商賈。蓋心無染著，慾界是仙都；心有繫戀，樂境成苦海矣。

To persist with fixed strong desires causes great pain. Sweetness is to put down and let them go.

Mountains and forests are delightful places, which, however, become marketplaces when people overly cling to them. Books and paintings are elegant objects, which, however, are transformed into merchandise when people are obsessed with them. To a person without strong fixed desires, even the most common place can be a paradise; otherwise, the paradise turns into a bitter ocean.

263、躁極則昏　靜極則明

時當喧雜，則平日所記憶者，皆漫然忘去；境在清寧，則夙昔所遺忘者，又恍爾現前。可見靜躁稍分，昏明頓異也。

Turmoil dulls senses. Tranquility sharpens intelligence.

Turmoil causes loss of memory; quite surroundings recall what has become dim. Likewise, when the heart is in turmoil, a person's senses become dull, but when the heart is in tranquility, his intelligence sharpened. The difference between turmoil and tranquility is the difference between intelligence and stupidity.

264、臥雲弄月　絕俗超塵

蘆花被下臥雪眠雲，保全得一窩夜氣；竹葉杯中吟風弄月，躲離了萬丈紅塵。

It is a divine feeling to enjoy the moon by lying on the clouds.

Enjoy a peaceful night by lying on the snow accompanied by the clouds and rushes. Escape worldly worries through drinking and constructing poems in the company of the moon and the wind.

265、鄙俗不及風雅　淡泊反勝濃厚

衰冕行中，著一個藜杖的山人，便增一段高風；漁樵路上，來一個袞衣的朝士，便添許多俗氣。固知濃不勝淡，俗不如雅也。

Worldly glamour is inferior to spiritual freedom. Simplicity is superior to sumptuousness.

Add a staff-holding mountain inhabitant to a group of magnificently dressed high government officials is to add a touch of spiritual freedom to the heavy bondage of wealth and power. Add a high government official in dignified uniform to a party of fishermen and lumberjacks is to add a touch of earthiness to natural grace. Worldly glamour is inferior to natural grace, and simplicity is superior to sumptuousness.

266、出世在涉世　了心在盡心

出世之道，即在涉世中，不必絕人以逃世；了心之功，即在盡心內，不必絕欲以灰心。

To study the great wisdom of enlightenment is to be involved in various social activities. To use the great wisdom to help people is to make the best efforts.

To study the great wisdom of enlightenment, people should involve themselves in various social activities instead of living alone in solitude. To use the great wisdom to help people, the person should make the best efforts to fulfill, instead of suppressing, this desire.

267、身放閒處　心在靜中

此身常放在閒處，榮辱得失誰能差遣我；此心常在安靜中，是非利害誰能瞞昧我。

Keep free both physically and spiritually.

He who is not busy himself with the worldly affairs will be moved neither by worldly gains nor loses. He who keeps his heart undisturbed by worldly desires will be blind to neither the right nor the wrong.

268、雲中世界　靜裡乾坤

竹籬下忽聞犬吠雞鳴，恍似雲中世界；芸窗中雅聽蟬吟燕語，方知靜裡乾坤。

The paradise is a world of peace.

Working by the bamboo hedge and accompanied by occasional barks and crows from afar, he cannot but wonder if he is in paradise. Reading in the study and enjoying the cheerful chattering of swallows and cicadas, one comes to realize the delight of a peaceful world.

269、不希榮達　不畏權勢

我不希榮，何憂乎利祿之香餌；我不競進，何畏乎世宦之危機。

Pursue neither glory nor success. Have fear for neither the powerful nor the influential.

Glory loses its attraction to those who do not long for it. The high government position poses no danger to the one who does not compete for it.

270、聖境之下　調心養神

徜徉於山林泉石之間，而塵心漸息；夷猶於詩書圖畫之內，而俗氣潛消。故君子雖不玩物喪志，亦常借境調心。

Refresh both mind and body in blissful surroundings.

Roaming among hills and streams purifies worldly desires. To be absorbed in books and paintings calms down the ambition for power and wealth. It is not recommended for any person to be overly indulged in hobbies, but it is highly recommended for all to refresh mind and body with proper recreation.

271、春之繁華　不若秋之清爽

春日氣象繁華，令人心神駘蕩，不若秋日雲白風清，蘭芳桂馥，水天一色，上下空明，使人神骨俱清也。

The flamboyant of spring cannot compare with the serenity of autumn.

The flamboyance of spring is intoxicating; but autumn, with its white clouds, gentle breeze, delightful orchid fragrance, pleasant cinnamon smell, clean water and clear sky, provides a quiet air of serenity. Serenity is better than flamboyance to purify a person both physically and spiritually.

272、得詩家真趣　悟禪教玄機

一字不識而有詩意者，得詩家真趣。一偈不參而有禪味者，悟禪教玄機。

Grasp the true spirit of poetry. Understand the subtle teachings of Zen Buddhism.

An illiterate is a real poet if he has grasped the true spirit of poetry. Even though he has never studied any of Zen's sacred writings, a common person is a real follower of Zen if he behaves according to Zen's subtle teachings.

273、像由心生　像隨心滅

機動的，弓影疑為蛇蠍，寢石視為伏虎，此中渾是殺氣；念息的，石虎可作海鷗，蛙聲可當鼓吹，觸處俱見真機。

The appearance and disappearance of an illusion is due to what is in the mind.

To those who are war thirsty, the shadow of a bow can be mistaken for a snake, and a still rock lying on the ground can be taken for a crouched tiger ready to attack. For them, malice pervades all places. To those who are with a peaceful nature, a savage tiger is looked upon as a sea gull, and the frog's croak is accepted as the melodious drumbeat. For them, peace is everywhere.

274、來去自如　融通自在

身如不繫之舟，一任流行坎止；心似既灰之木，何妨刀割香塗。

Be neither entangled nor confined. Feel at ease with whatever the situation may be.

The tangible body is like a floating boat without being tied up on the anchor. Its movement follows the current without a fixed destination. The intangible heart is like the cold ashes of burned wood. It will be affected neither by painful knife cuts nor by comfortable soothing balm.

275、憂喜取捨之情　皆是形氣用事

人情聽鶯啼則喜，聞蛙鳴則厭，見花則思培之，遇草則欲去之，俱是以形氣用事；若以性天視之，何者非自鳴其天機，非自暢其生意也。

Human emotions reflect subjective feelings.

People are happy upon hearing the oriole's songs, but feel annoyed with the frog's croaks. They feel pleased to see beautiful flowers and wish to cultivate them, but are disgusted to see weeds and wish to get rid of them. These are all subjective human reactions. From the natural point of view, the sound of oriole and that of frog are the same, for both sing the song of life; and the flower and the weed are alike, for both display the color and form of life.

276、夢幻空華　真如之月

髮落齒疏，任幻形之凋謝；鳥吟花開，識本性之真如。

Recognize the difference between the illusory and the real.

The physical body is but the illusion of life. There is no need to feel sorry when hair turns thin and teeth become loose. What is the reality of life? The bird's nature is to sing. The flower's nature is to bloom. Therefore, to sing is the reality of bird's life and to bloom the flower's life. When the bird stops singing, it stops living. When the flower ceases to bloom, it ceases to live. The reality of a person's life is his true nature. Only when a person has recognized his true nature and behaved accordingly, does he actually live in this world.

277、欲心生邪念　虛心生正念

欲其中者，波沸寒潭，山林不見其寂；虛其中者，涼生酷暑，朝市不知其喧。

Undue desires breed evil thoughts. Good thoughts will develop when undue desires are driven away.

When a person is dominated by undue desires, he is like a calm pond disturbed fiercely by high waves. It will be difficult for him to find inner tranquility although he retreats to the deep forest on a high mountain. When a person bans undue desires from his heart, he will find cool and refreshing air even in hot mid-summer days. His inner tranquility will not be disturbed although he lives in the middle of a noisy market place.

278、富者多憂　貴者多險

多藏者厚亡，故知富不如貧之無慮；高步者疾顛，故知貴不如賤之常安。

The rich are also rich in worries. The powerful are often plagued with powerful dangers.

The poor have fewer worries than the rich, for those who store abundantly lose abundantly too. The one who is high up on the social ladder enjoys less peace than the one on the lower rank, for people who are high up fall easier and heavier.

279、讀易松間　談經竹下

讀易曉窗，丹砂研松間之露；談經午案，寶磬宣竹下之風。

Study *Book of Changes* among pine trees. Discuss Buddhist scriptures under bamboos.

At dawn, it would be wonderful to study *Book of Changes* among pine trees and to mark the important parts with the red ink mixed with the dew drippings from the pines. At noon, it would be divine to read Buddhist scriptures under bamboos and to tap the precious musical stone to preach the passing winds.

280、人為乏生趣　天機在自然

花居盆內終乏生機，鳥入籠中便減天趣，不若山間花鳥錯集成文，翱翱自若，無不悠然會心。

The human design lacks vitality. Heaven's messages lie in nature.

Potted flowers lack vitality. Caged birds lack vigor. Flowers and birds in nature weave a beautiful and lively picture to carry Heaven's messages to people.

281、煩惱由我起　嗜好自心生

世人只緣認得我字太真，故多種種嗜好，種種煩惱。前人云：不復知有我，安知物為貴。又云：知身不是我，煩惱更何侵。真破的之言也。

Worries come from ego. Weakness comes from undue desires.

People often over emphasize their own importance and thus attract various worries and form different weaknesses. An old Chinese saying tells us: "The material value disappears with the disappearance of the physical body. To ignore oneself is to ignore material values." Another goes, "When a person realizes the illusive nature of his physical body, worries cannot find a footing in him." How wise these words are!

282、以失意之思　制得意之念

自老視少，可以消奔馳角逐之心；自瘁視榮，可以絕粉華靡麗之念。

Suppress the desire for success with the prospect of its gloomy result.

A young person will not exert himself to pursue power and wealth if he understands that they will prevent neither the deterioration nor the misery of old age. People will not go out of way to covet a sumptuous way of life if they are aware that the ending of its short span is pain and distress.

283、世態變化無極　萬事必須達觀

人情世態，倏忽萬端，不宜認得太真。堯夫*云：昔日所云我，而今卻是伊，不知今日我，又屬後來誰。人能常作如是觀，便可解卻胸中罥矣。

As the world turns so does everything else. Don't take things too seriously.

Everything in the world is subject to rapid changes. Human relationships are especially fickle. There is no need to take changes too seriously. Mr. Shao Yong (10ll-1077), a wise and learned scholar in the Song Dynasty, said, "Yesterday's I has become today's he. Who will be today's I tomorrow."If everybody would think the way Mr. Sao thought, worry would disappear.

284、鬧中取靜　冷處熱心

熱鬧中著一冷眼，便省許多苦心思；冷落處存一熱心，便得許多真趣味。

Be cool and calm in heated exhilaration. Be warm and enthusiastic when sadly deserted.

Be cool and calm in heated exhilaration, and many nasty troubles can be prevented. Be warm and enthusiastic when sadly deserted, and many life's true tastes will be revealed.

---

* 邵雍（10ll-1077）：字堯夫，號安樂先生，諡康節，宋朝理學家。

285、世間原無絕對　安樂只是尋常

有一樂境界，就有一不樂的相對待；有一好光景，就有一不好的相乘除。只是尋常家飯，素味風光，才是個安樂的窩巢。

Nothing is absolute in the world. Ordinary daily life leads to perpetual peace and happiness.

While there is happiness, there is sorrow as a contrast; and great success goes hand in hand with great failure. Ordinary homemade meals and simple daily life are the essential elements for a perpetual peaceful and happy life.

286、接近自然風光　物我歸於一如

簾櫳高敞，看青山綠水吞吐雲煙，識乾坤之自在；竹樹扶疏，任乳燕鳴鳩送迎時序，知物我之兩忘。

Be close to nature where everything lives harmoniously.

It will dawn on us that this universe is peaceful and carefree when we roll up the bamboo window screen to see green mountains and blue waters breathing in and out white clouds and mists. We will realize that we human beings and everything else in nature belong to one big harmonious family as we watch baby swallows and singing pigeons bidding greetings and farewells to different seasons.

287、生死成敗　一任自然

知成之必敗，則求成之心不必太堅；知生之必死，則保生之道不必過勞。

Let everything in the world take its natural course.

Since all achievements are doomed to be superseded, there is no need to seek achievement with iron determination. Since death is inevitable for every life, there is no need to take great pains to keep alive.

288、處世流水落花　身心皆得自在

古德云：竹影掃階塵不動，月輪穿沼水無痕；吾儒云：水流任急境常靜，花落雖頻意自閒。人常持此意，以應事接物，身心何等自在。

Conduct life the way as the falling flowers or the flowing water. Keep both body and mind free and at ease.

Wise Buddhists have taught us, "When the shadow of bamboo sweeps over the steps, it does not move any dust. When the reflection of the moon floats over the water, it does not leave any trace." Knowledgeable Confucians also have said, "Though water rushes, its surroundings remain calm and quiet. Though flowers keep on falling, the atmosphere is peaceful and relaxed." Conduct life the way as the falling flowers or the rushing water, and both body and mind will be free and at ease.

289、勘破乾坤妙趣　識見天地文章

林間松韻，石上泉聲，靜裡聽來，識天地自然鳴佩；草際煙光，水心雲影，閒中觀去，見乾坤最上文章。

Know the real joy of the universe. Recognize the best compositions of Heaven and Earth.

Listen quietly to the sound of wind passing through pines and to the babble of the spring running over rocks. They are the songs of Heaven and Earth. Observe idly the smoky light among grasses and the shadow of clouds in the water. They are the best compositions in the universe.

290、猛獸易服　人心難制

眼看西晉之荊榛，猶矜白刃；身屬北邙之狐兔，尚惜黃金。語云：猛獸易服，人心難降；谿壑易填，人心難滿。信哉。

Wild animals are easy to tame. Human desires are difficult to suppress.

When the Western Jin Dynasty was about to be overthrown, its government officials still blindly believed in strong military forces. Even though their bodies will soon be in the bellies of wild foxes and rabbits in the graveyard on North Mountain, people are still greedy for gold. An old Chinese saying goes: "Wild animals are easy to tame, but not human desires. Vast gorges are easy to fill up, but not human's avarice." How true it is!

291、心地能平穩安靜　觸處皆青山綠水

心地上無風濤，隨在皆青山綠樹；性天中有化育，觸處都魚躍鳶飛。

When the mind is peaceful, there are green mountains and blue water everywhere.

When there is no storm in our mind, everywhere we go there are pleasant mountains and beautiful trees. When there is goodwill in our heart, everywhere we look are kites flying and fishes jumping.

292、生活自適其性　貴人不若平民

峨冠大帶之士，一旦睹輕簑小笠飄飄然逸也，未必不動其諮嗟；長筵廣席之豪，一旦遇疏簾淨几悠悠焉靜也，未必不增其綣戀。人奈何驅以火牛，誘以風馬，而不思自適其性哉。

The life of a commoner agrees better with human nature than that of a nobleman.

A noble man with his high-topped hat and wide waist band cannot but envy those who wear only a light coir raincoat and a plain bamboo hat. The rich man with his long-lasting and pompous feasts cannot but envy those who sit peacefully in a room with a simple bamboo screen and a clean desk. Why do people fight against their nature to seek material glories instead of living a peaceful and natural life?

293、處世忘世　超物樂天

遊魚不知海，飛鳥不知空；識此可以超物累，可以樂天機。

Live in the world but not try to possess it. Be free from material bondage and enjoy what we have.

Fishes swimming in the water never feel that there is any need to hoard water. Birds flying in the sky never claim that the sky is their property. To understand this concept is to be free from material bondage and to happily enjoy what Heaven provides us.

294、人生本無常　盛衰何可恃

狐眠敗砌，兔走荒台，盡是當年歌舞之地；露冷黃花，煙迷衰草，悉屬舊時爭戰之場。盛衰何常，強弱安在。念此，令人心灰。

Life is fickle. Its ups and downs are undependable.

Deserted buildings where foxes sleep and desolate porches where rabbits haunt were places for singing and dancing in old days. Occupied by cold-dew-drenched wild yellow flowers and chilly-mist-enveloped withered grasses, the field was the hot battlefield in days gone-by. Where are the past glories and humiliations? Few people will not feel disheartened on thinking of this question.

295、寵辱不驚　去留無意

寵辱不驚，閒看庭前花開花落；去留無意，漫隨天外雲卷雲舒。

Accept honor and disgrace with the same peaceful attitude. Hold or drop a prestigious position without a set idea.

Accepting honor and disgrace with the same peaceful attitude as when leisurely observing flowers in their ups and downs in the front yard. Holding or dropping a prestigious position should be treated with the same easy manner as when watching the changes of the clouds in the sky.

296、苦海茫茫　回頭是岸

晴空朗月，何處不可翱翔，而飛蛾獨投夜燭；清泉綠草，何物不可飲啄，而鴟鴞偏嗜腐鼠。噫，世之不為飛蛾鴟鴞者，幾何人哉。

The ocean of distress is boundless. If a person is willing to turn back, the shore of salvation is right at hand.

The clear sky with the bright moon provides a vast safe space, but the flying moth commits suicide by throwing itself into the candle flame. The clean streams and the green fields yield a huge variety of foods, but the owl stuffs itself with rotten stinking rats. Alas! How many people in this world are not acting like the flying moth and the owl?

297、求心內之佛　卻心外之法

才就筏便思舍筏，方是無事道人；若騎驢又復覓驢，終為不了禪師。

Abandon written scriptures to find Buddha within the heart.

To a traveler, the destination, not the boat, should be the main concern of his mind. To a person seeking for enlightenment, the teachings revealed by the written words in scriptures, not the written words, should be his chief pursuit. If a seeker sets his mind on the written words instead, he is like a rider who rides on the donkey but still looks for it. It is impossible for him to become an enlightened master. After all, Buddha is in everyone's heart not in the world outside.

298、以冷情當事　如湯之消雪

權貴龍驤，英雄虎戰，以冷眼視之，如蟻聚羶，如蠅競血；是非蜂起，得失蝟興，以冷情當之，如冶化金，如湯消雪。

Be calm in handling problems, and problems will be resolved like snow melted by hot water.

The powerful and wealthy proudly show their mighty forces, and the heroic fight fiercely for the final victory. In the eyes of a calm bystander, they are but like the ants that gather on the smelly meat, or flies that race for stinky blood. All sorts of disputes and conflicts, if handled calmly, will be resolved smoothly and quickly like snow melted by hot water and gold tempered by fire.

299、徹見真性　自達聖境

羈鎖於物欲，覺吾生之可哀；夷猶於性真，覺吾生之可樂。知其可哀，則塵情立破；知其可樂，則聖境自臻。

After the true nature of life is fully understood, a happy and peaceful state reveals itself at once.

Life is miserable when bound by undue desires, but joyful when it follows its genuine nature. When the moment a person recognizes the root of misery, he is free from bondage at once. As soon as a person identifies the source of joy, he obtains heavenly peace in no time.

300、心月開朗　水月無礙

胸中即無半點物欲，已如雪消爐焰冰消日；眼前自有一段空明，時見月在青天影在波。

When the moon in a person's heart is clear of any shadow, so will its reflection in his life.

When a person's undue desires vanish completely like snow in fire and ice under the sun, he will be free of worries and feel at ease. After all, when the luminous moon appears in the clear sky, its spotless reflection in the water can be surely counted on.

301、野趣豐處　詩興自湧

詩思在灞陵橋上，微吟就，林岫便已浩然；野興在鏡湖曲邊，獨往時，山川自相映發。

Poetic inspiration comes spontaneously in natural surroundings.

Walking on a picturesque bridge, one is seized by a sudden urge to compose a poem, which is endorsed overwhelmingly at once by the entire company of woods and mountains. Strolling alone by a clear lake, one cannot but fall in love with the natural beauty of mountains and waters. Indeed, nature itself is a piece of incomparable picture and poem.

302、見微知著　守正待時

伏久者飛必高，開先者謝獨早。知此，可以免蹭蹬之憂，可以消躁急之念。

Concealed features can be detected from trifles. Insist upon moral principles to wait for the right moment to come.

Birds that can lie long in ambush are able to fly high. Flowers that bloom early wither early. These are good examples to tell us to be patient for the right moment to come.

303、森羅萬象　夢幻泡影

樹木至歸根日，而後知華萼枝葉之徒榮；人事至蓋棺時，而後知子女玉帛之無益。

Various phenomena of the universe are but illusive dreams and bubble shadows.

Only when its root dries up, does the tree realize that beautiful flowers and lush leaves are but useless vanity. Only when his coffin is sealed, does a person understand that offspring and wealth are but futile bubble shadows.

304、在世出世　真空不空

真空不空，執相非真，破相亦非真，問世尊如何發付？在世出世，徇欲是苦，絕欲亦是苦，聽吾儕善自修持。

The way to escape from this world is to stay in this world. To have no desires is not to abstain from desires all together.

To have no desires is not to abstain from desires all together. To hold on material value is not correct, but to reject material value completely is not correct either. What a puzzle! Gautama Buddha, please point out a clear direction for me to follow. Escaping from this world is not the key for a happy life. Instead, one should face worldly problems courageously and try to solve them. Both indulging in undue desires and abstain from desires totally cause great pain. Only when a person successfully clears away the undue desires and insists upon the good ones, will he find happiness. The answer is in individual's hands.

305、欲望雖有尊卑　貪爭並無二致

　　烈士讓千乘，貪夫爭一文，人品星淵也，而好名不殊好利；天子營家國，乞人號饔餐，分位霄壤也，而焦思何異焦聲。

Desires can be classified in many different types, but their avarice and contending nature is the same.

　　There are two persons: a hero who turns down a feudal prince position that entitles him to possess one thousand chariots and a greedy man who fights over a penny. The difference of their moral characters is giant. However, there is little difference in the avarice for a good name and the avarice for a good monetary profit. There are two persons: a king who runs a country and a beggar who cries for food. As for their social status, the difference is huge. However, there is little difference in the anxiety of ruling the country successfully and the anxiety of obtaining enough food.

306、毀譽褒貶　一任世情

　　飽諳世味，一任覆雨翻雲，總慵開眼；會盡人情，隨教呼牛喚馬，只是點頭。

Accept whatever the world chooses to say about us, whether it is high praise or harsh criticism.

　　Having experienced various tastes of the world, an enlightened person is too lazy to pay any attention to the most unstable human affection. Having gone through various forms of human snobbishness, an enlightened person answers to whatever name people choose to call him without the least objection.

307、不為念想囚繫　凡事皆要隨緣

今人專求無念，而終不可無。只是前念不滯，後念不迎，但將現在的隨緣打發得去，自然漸漸入無。

Don't be bound by undue desires. Let everything follow its natural course.

People strive to drive away undue desires, but undue desires persist. In fact, undue desires will gradually fade away when people refuse to keep the old, welcome not the new, and dispel the current according to their natural courses.

308、自然得真機　造作減趣味

意所偶會便成佳境，物出天然才見真機，若加一分調停佈置，趣味便減矣。白氏*云：意隨無事適，風逐自然清。其言之也。

Everything in its natural state is genuinely pleasant. Any artificial modification diminishes its joyful nature.

When a momentary impulse is fulfilled by chance, it is delightful. Everything in its natural state is genuinely pleasant. Any artificial modification spoils the joyful elements. Bai Juyi (772-846), a well-known poet in the Tang Dynasty, said, "The mind is peaceful when it is without any fixed desire. The wind is fair when it dances following its nature."

---

* 白居易（772-846）：字樂天，唐代著名詩人。

309、徹見自性　不必談禪

性天澄徹，即飢餐渴飲，無非康濟身心；心地沉迷，縱談禪演偈，總是播弄精魄。

Zen becomes superfluous when life's true nature is found.

Eat when hungry, and drink when thirsty. This is life's simple but genuine nature. If a person is possessed by undue desires, he will be able to find neither spiritual peace nor physical health even though he discusses and practices Zen all day long.

310、心境恬淡　絕慮忘憂

人心有個真境，非絲非竹而自恬愉，不煙不茗而自清芬，須念淨境空，慮忘形釋，才得以遊衍其中。

Simplicity and contentment keep worries away.

The heart's genuine state is peaceful and happy. It arrives only when a person has successfully banned undue desires and has freed himself from both mental anxiety and physical fatigue. Any other methods, such as playing music and burning incense, are futile.

311、真不離幻　雅不離俗

金自礦出，玉從石生，非幻無以求真；道得酒中，仙遇花裡，雖雅不能離俗。

Reality cannot be separated from vision. The heavenly cannot be parted from the mundane.

Gold comes from ore and jade from rock. Without vision, reality is beyond reach. People are enlightened through wine and find bliss among flowers. They all explain that the heavenly cannot be separated from the worldly.

312、凡俗差別觀　道心一體觀

天地中萬物，人倫中萬情，世界中萬事，以俗眼觀，紛紛各異，以道眼觀，種種是常，何須分別，何須取捨。

Everything in the universe is different from the mundane point of view, but from Tao's point of view, the same truth applies to all.

Numerous creatures in the universe, various relationships of human beings , and different happenings on the earth are all confusingly different from the mundane point of view. However, from Tao's point of view, everything in the world lives by the same truth. There is no need to differentiate or to choose one from another.

313、布茅蔬淡　頤養天和

神酣布被窩中，得天地沖和之氣；味足藜羹飯後，識人生淡泊之真。

Coarse cotton and common vegetables nurture heavenly peace.

A good and restful sleep in a coarse cotton blanket provides heavenly peace to the sleeper. After a solid common vegetable meal, the enlightened one realizes that simple life is the true joy on earth.

314、了心悟性　俗即是僧

纏脫只在自心，心了則屠肆糟廛，居然淨土。不然，縱一琴一鶴一花一卉，嗜好雖清，魔障終在。語云：能休，塵境為真境；未了，僧家是俗家。信夫。

After clearing out undue desires to recover life's true nature, an ordinary common person is a divine monk.

To be bound by undue desires or not depends absolutely on individual. To those who choose to be free from undue desires, a slaughterhouse or a noisy tavern can be peaceful and heavenly. To those who choose to stay in bondage, even the simple and peaceful hobbies such as playing instruments, keeping a pet, or growing flowers can be a source of great trouble and many worries. An old Chinese saying goes, "When a person puts down his undue desires, his world turns from earthly to heavenly. Failing in doing so, even a divine monk remains earthly bound.

315、斷絕思慮　光風霽月

斗室中，萬慮都捐，說甚畫棟飛雲，珠簾捲雨；三杯後，一真自得，唯知素琴橫月，短笛吟風。

Get rid of worries to make room for the bright moon and the gentle wind.

After having put down all worries, an enlightened person will rather live in a simple little room than in a lavishly decorated mansion. After having found the true nature of life, the enlightened person amuses himself with a few cups of wine, and finds joy in playing the simple stringed instrument to the moon or playing the flute to the wind.

316、機神觸事　應物而發

萬籟寂寥中，忽聞一鳥弄聲，便喚起許多幽趣；萬卉摧剝後，忽持一枝擢秀，便觸動無限生機。可見性天未常枯槁，機神最宜觸發。

Enlightenment comes from various sources at the right moment with the least effort.

A bird's chirping in the dark silent night awakens boundless joy. The first flower after the severe winter triggers unlimited hope for life. Nature is not dead or dry. Instead, it provides endless hope for joy and life.

317、操持身心　收放自如

白氏云：「不如放身心，冥然任天造。」晁氏*云：「不如收身心，凝然歸寂定。」放者流為猖狂，收者入於枯寂。唯善操身心者，欛柄在手，收放自如。

Conduct life properly without going to extremes.

The Tang Dynasty poet Bai Juyi (772~846) said, "Let the heart go free. Let the heart follows its natural course." The famous Song Dynasty scholar Chao Buzhi (1053-1110) held different opinion by saying, "Discipline the heart to be serene." Those who let the heart go completely free are apt to become wild and impudent. Those who discipline the heart with strict rules easily become dry and dull. Only those who are masters of their desires can be free and serene at the proper moment.

318、自然人心　融和一體

當雪夜月天，心境便爾澄澈；遇春風和氣，意界亦自沖融。造化人心，混合無間。

Nature and the human heart merge into one.

In a white snowy night with the luminous moon in the sky, people are easy to feel tranquil and peaceful. When gentle spring winds bring mild weather to the world, people are apt to be pleasant and amiable. Nature and the human heart merge into one.

---

* 晁補之（1053-1110）：宋進士，工書畫，著有《雞肋集》等書。

319、不弄技巧　以拙為進

文以拙進，道以拙成，一拙字有無限意味；如桃源犬吠，桑間雞鳴，何等淳龐。至於寒潭之月，古木之鴉，工巧中便覺有衰颯氣象矣。

Be rather crude and honest than crafty and clever.

Crudeness is the key word in improving both writing ability and moral character. Being crude is an honest reflection of truth, and that is appealing. The dog's bark in the countryside and the cock's crow among mulberry trees depict a crude but true picture of country life that is simple and lively. However, the moon in a cold deep pond and the raven on a withered old tree provide a cunningly arranged artificial setting that is crafty and dismal.

320、以我轉物　逍遙自在

以我轉物者，得固不喜，失亦不憂，大地盡屬逍遙；以物役我者，逆固生憎，順亦生愛，一毛便生纏縛。

Be the master of desires. Be carefree.

Being the master of his desires, a person will be affected neither by success nor failure. The world is a paradise to him, and he is free to enjoy everything in it. Being the slave of his desires, a person reacts strongly to ups and downs. To him, the world is an ocean of distress, and a mere trifle can cause endless pain.

321、形影皆去　心境皆空

理寂則事寂，遣事執理者，似去影留形；心空則境空，去境存心者，如聚羶卻蚋。

Keep neither concrete shapes nor illusory shadows. Clear out undue desires to keep worries away.

The relation between theory and practice is like the shape and its shadow. Persist in a theory without practice is empty, so is keeping the shape without its shadow. Since undue desires are causes for all worries, worries will disappear with the removal of undue desires. When the heart is empty of undue desires, worries will disappear accordingly. Keeping undue desires with the hope to repel distress is like to gather smelly meat with the hope to repel gnats.

322、任其自然　萬事安樂

幽人韻事，總在自適，故酒以不勸為歡，棋以不爭為勝，笛以無腔為適，琴以無弦為高，會以不期約為真率，客以不迎送為坦夷。若一牽文泥跡，便落塵世苦海矣。

Let everything be, and everything is at peace and happy.

A delightful activity consists basically in its agreeable nature: drinking without being warmly forced, playing chess but not competing to win, playing the flute but not required in tune, playing the stringed instrument but not necessary on the right strings, visiting friends but not making appointments in advance, and receiving guests but not observing rigid rules of propriety. It brings only pain not joy when the activity is bound with any sign of formality.

323、思及生死　萬念灰冷

試思未生之前，有何象貌，又思既死之後，作何景色，則萬念灰冷，一性寂然，自可超物外，遊象先矣。

The thought of life and death brings all worldly desires to an end.

What was it like before birth? What will it be after death? These questions will certainly put people's worldly desires to an end. Without undue desires, a person would be able to roam the world and enjoy a carefree life.

324、卓智之人　洞燭機先

遇病而後思健之為寶，處亂而後思平之為福，非早智也；倖福而知其為禍之本，貪生而知其為死之因，其卓見乎。

A wise person anticipates fortunes both good and bad.

Those who appreciate good health after illness and value peace after war are not wise. Those who detect disaster in undeserved good fortune and sense death in the life of a cowardly nature possess supreme wisdom.

325、雌雄妍醜　一時假相

優人傅粉調朱，效妍醜於毫端，俄而歌殘場罷，妍醜何存；奕者爭先競後，較雌雄於枰間，俄而局盡子收，雌雄安在。

Success and failure are but temporary illusions.

Actors and actresses do their best to make up with powder and rouge to impersonate the beautiful and the ugly on stage. When the curtain falls down, so do the beautiful and the ugly. Chess players fight fiercely against each other on the chessboard. When the game is over, so are the winners and the losers.

326、風月木石之真趣　惟靜與閒者得之

風花之瀟灑，雪月之空清，唯靜者為之主；水木之榮枯，竹石之消長，獨閒者識其真。

Only the one with inner peace and the one with leisure time can truly appreciate the beauty in nature.

It takes a person with inner peace to appreciate the grace of the flower, the freedom of the wind, the brightness of the moon, and the purity of the snow. It takes a person with leisure time to recognize the relationship of water and plants and the interaction between rocks and bamboo bushes.

327、天全欲淡　雖凡亦仙

田父野叟，語以黃雞白酒則欣然喜，問以鼎食則不知；語以緼袍短褐則油然樂，問以袞服則不識。其天全，故其欲淡，此是人生第一個境界。

Simple and common people without undue desires are truly blessed.

Farmers and woodchoppers are glad to discuss simple daily food, such as home-raised chicken and home-brewed wine, but feel lost on the subject of luxurious feasts. They are happy to talk about ordinary daily clothing, such as old cotton robes and coarse working shorts, but feel blank on the subject of expensive official outfits. They are blessed with the secrets of happiness on earth: simplicity and contentment.

328、本真即佛　何待觀心

心無其心，何有於觀。釋氏曰，觀心者，重增其障。物本一物，何待於齊。莊生*曰，齊物者，自剖其同。

When a person's heart is in its original state, he is divine. There is no need to introspect.

There is no need for a person to introspect when his heart is in its original state void of any undue desires. When Buddha asks people to practice introspection, he adds a heavy burden on them. All things in the universe are but one. When Zhuangzi (ca. 369-ca. 286 BC), the great master of Taoism, said that people should treat everything in the universe equally, he differentiates what is the same.

---

* 莊周（約西元前369－西元前286）：戰國時宋國蒙人。其人生觀順應自然，社會觀歸於無治，與老子並為道家思想的宗師，著有《莊子》一書。

329、勿待興盡　適可而止

　　笙歌正濃處，便自拂衣長往，見達人撒手懸崖；更漏已殘時，猶然夜行不休，笑俗士沉身苦海。

Don't indulge to the utmost of your heart's desire. To stop at a proper moment is wise.

The one who leaves at the peak of a party is admirable, for he knows to retreat from the dangerous cliff in time. He who keeps burning the candle at both ends even at very late hours is lamentable, for he is in an ocean of endless distress.

330、修行宜絕跡於塵寰　悟道當涉足於世俗

　　把握未定，宜絕跡塵囂，使此心不見可欲而不亂，以澄吾靜體；操持既堅，又當混跡風塵，使此心見可欲而亦不亂，以養吾圓機。

Keep away from mundane temptations to cultivate moral character. Participate in mundane activities after enlightenment.

Before a strong moral character has been successfully molded, keep away from mundane temptations, lest the mind be disturbed. After the moral character has been well formed, take part in mundane activities to confirm the reliability of repelling temptations and to further develop wisdom.

331、人我一空　動靜兩忘

喜寂厭喧者，往往避人以求靜。不知意在無人，便成我相，心著於靜，便是動根，如何到得人我一空，動靜兩忘的境界。

Merge into the world and interfered by neither noise nor silence.

An introvert prefers to be alone and tries to avoid people to be quiet. Longing to avoid people is a desire, and wishing to be quietly alone is a motive. With the motive and the desire in mind, how can he successfully reach the state of tranquility?

332、山居清灑　入都俗氣

山居胸次清灑，觸物皆有佳思：見孤雲野鶴，而起超絕之想；遇石澗流泉，而動澡雪之思；撫老檜寒梅，而勁節挺立；侶沙鷗麋鹿，而機心頓忘。若一走入塵寰，無論物不相關，即此身亦屬贅旒矣。

People find heavenly inspiration in the mountain but mundane burden in the city.

People enjoy heavenly life in the mountain. Everything there is an incentive to good thinking: a lonely cloud or a wild crane inspires lofty and noble thoughts. The brook breaking on rocks encourages snowy white ideas. Chinese upright old cypresses or the snow-endured plum blossoms set good examples of not bending to the wicked. Gentle deer and peaceful gulls help people forget the tricks and deceptions in the world. In the city, even though not involved in any mundane affairs, body itself is like the superfluous fringe.

333、人我合一之時　則雲留而鳥伴

興逐時來，芳草地撒履閒行，野鳥忘機時作伴；景與心會，落花下披襟兀坐，白雲無語漫相留。

When a person merges into nature, the cloud lingers and birds become his good companions.

Kicking off shoes to take a leisurely walk on grass, the person who becomes a part of nature finds wild birds come to be his company. Sitting alone with blossoms falling on his casually dressed robe, the person who merges into nature finds the white cloud quietly lingers over his head to invite him to stay.

334、禍福苦樂　一念之差

人生福境禍區，皆念想造成。故釋氏云：利欲熾然，即是火坑；貪愛沉溺，便為苦海；一念清淨，烈焰成池；一念驚覺，船登彼岸。念頭稍異，境界頓殊，可不慎哉。

A minute difference in thinking will decide fortune or misfortune and happiness or distress.

A person's thinking decides a person's fortune. Buddha says: "Burning desire is the furnace with blazing fire. Foolish indulgence is the ocean of distress. Putting down the burning desire converts immediately a hot burning furnace into a cool refreshing pool. Turning away from indulgence brings instantly a drowning person to the land of safety." A minute difference in thinking produces a vast different result. Should people not be careful?

335、若要工夫深　鐵杵磨成針

繩鋸木斷，水滴石穿，學道者須加努力；水到渠成，瓜熟蒂落，得道者一任天機。

With persistent efforts, an iron bar can be ground into a sewing needle.

Just as the rope can saw a log into two, and the dripping water can wear through a rock; so those who wish to learn Tao should be patient and never give up. Just as the water forms a passage easily when it comes, and the melon falls naturally when it is ripe; so those who wish to learn Tao should keep in mind that after adequate effort, they will obtain Tao smoothly at the right moment.

336、機息心清　月到風來

機息時，便有月到風來，不必苦海人世；心遠處，自無車塵馬跡，何須痼疾丘山。

When the mind is free from trickery, the heart can feel the gentle breeze and the bright moon.

An honest person is blessed with peace. His life is safe from the ocean of distress. The person who is indifferent to worldly glory will not attract flatterers. There is no need for him to live as a seriously sick person who has to live on some remote mountain to recuperate.

337、落葉蘊育萌芽　生機藏於肅殺

　　草木才零落，便露萌穎於根底；時序雖凝寒，終回陽氣於飛灰。肅殺之中，生生之意常為之主，即是可以見天地之心。

Fallen leaves fertilize young sprouts. Life is conceived in death.

Roots produce new sprouts the same time when the leaves fall. Even in severe winter, hope for the warm sun always exists. The fact that life is never absent from what is barren and harsh proves that Heaven and Earth is merciful.

338、雨後山色鮮　靜夜鐘聲清

　　雨餘觀山色，景象更覺新妍；夜靜聽鐘聲，音響尤為清越。

The color of the mountain is fresher after rain. The sound of the bell is clearer in a quiet night.

The mountain assumes fresher and brighter hue after rain. The bell sounds clearer and carries farther in a quiet night.

339、雪夜讀書神清　登山眺望心曠

登高使人心曠，臨流使人意遠，讀書於雨雪之夜，使人神清，舒嘯於丘阜之巔，使人興邁。

Studying in a snowy night awakens mind. The distant prospect on a high mountain frees people from spiritual bondage.

People feel carefree on a high mountain, thoughtful by the running stream, clear-headed when studying in a snowy night, and elated when shouting on the hill top.

340、萬鐘一髮　存乎一心

心曠，則萬鐘如瓦罐。心隘，則一髮似車輪。

The value of a million-dollar position and a thread of hair depends on how one views them.

To the generous and big-hearted, a million-dollar position is as worthless as an earthen jar. To the mean and hard-hearted, a thread of hair is as valuable as a giant wheel.

341、要以我轉物　勿以物役我

無風月花柳，不成造化。無情欲嗜好，不成心體；只以我轉物，不以物役我，則嗜慾莫非天機，塵情即是理境矣。

Be the master of desires not the slave.

Without love and mating, it is impossible for Mother Nature to produce life. When devoid of desire and feeling, it is unlikely for a person to be a complete entity. However, it is important to be the master of one's desire not the slave. If a person keeps his desire under proper control, his desire becomes the messenger from Heaven, and what is worldly becomes heavenly.

342、就身了身　以物付物

就一身了一身者，方能以萬物付萬物；還天下於天下者，方能出世間於世間。

Fully understand your capacity. Share the universe with whatever is in it.

Only when a person fully understands his limitations and takes on only what is within his capacity, is he able to share the universe with whatever is in it. Only when a person stops taking the world as his personal belongings, is he able to live a divine and happy life on the earth.

343、不可徒勞身心　當樂風月之趣

人生太閒，則別念竊生；太忙，則真性不現。故士君子不可不抱身心之憂，亦不可不耽風月之趣。

All work and no play make a person dull and dry.

While too much spare time gives birth to evil thoughts, too little suffocates a person's liveliness. An enlightened person should find balance between work and play.

344、何處無妙境　何處無淨土

人心多從動處失真。若一念不生，澄然靜坐，雲興而悠然共逝，雨滴而冷然俱清，鳥啼而欣然有會，花落而瀟然自得。何地非真境，何物無真機。

Paradise is everywhere, so is peace and joy.

Troubles arise with undue desires. A person who does not have any undue desire is at peace with himself, and he will be able to drift freely with the idle cloud, to appreciate the cooling dripping rain-drops, to communicate with the singing bird, and to learn from the graceful falling flowers. To him, paradise is everywhere, and everything shows him its natural beauty.

345、順逆一視　欣戚兩忘

子生而母危，鏹積而盜窺，何喜非憂也。貧可以節用，病可以保身，何憂非喜也。故達人當順逆一視，而欣戚兩忘。

Accept adversity and good fortune with the same attitude. Be affected by neither happiness nor sorrow.

A mother is in great danger when she gives birth to a baby. Great wealth attracts thieves and robbers. Is there any happiness that is totally free from the shadow of sorrow? Poverty teaches people to be thrifty, and illness warns people to take good care of their health. What sorrow does not lead to good fortune? An enlightened person accepts both adversity and good fortune with the same attitude, and is affected by neither happiness nor sorrow.

346、風跡月影　過而不留

耳根似飆谷投響，過而不留，則是非俱謝；心境如月池浸色，空而不著，則物我兩忘。

Keep neither the echo of the high wind nor the shadow of the moon.

The echo of the high wind fills up the whole valley but leaves no trace at all after it passes through. When gossips and rumors we hear are treated in this way, troubles can be avoided. The moonlight changes the color of the entire pond but fails to change the water's true nature. If we meet ups and downs in life similarly, the tranquility of the heart can be retained.

347、世間皆樂　苦自心生

世人為榮利纏縛，動曰塵世苦海，不知雲白山青，川行石立，花迎鳥笑，谷答樵謳，世亦不塵，海亦不苦，彼自塵苦其心爾。

The world is full of joy. Sorrow comes from the undue desire.

Those who are bound by worldly fame and wealth complain that this world is a dusty land and an ocean of distress. They are blind and deaf to the white cloud floating over the green mountain, the standing rock seeing off the running brook, the smiling flower greeting the singing bird, and the deep valley echoing the woodchopper's song. The world is not dusty, and the ocean is not bitter. It is people who trouble themselves with dust and agony.

348、月盈則虧　履滿者戒

花看半開，酒飲微醉，此中大有佳趣。若至爛漫酕醄，便成惡境矣。履盈滿者，宜思之。

A full moon is on its way to wane. Those who are at the zenith of his success should keep this lesson in mind.

A half- opened flower and the state of tipsiness are both charming, but a flower overblown or a person deadly drunk becomes a nightmare. He who is at the zenith of his success should bear this lesson in mind.

349、體任自然　不染世法

　　山肴不受世間灌溉，野禽不受世間豢養，其味皆香而且冽。吾人能不為世法所點染，其臭味不迥然別乎。

Follow what is natural. Don't be contaminated by mundane opinion.

The taste of wild vegetables and wild animals not raised by human beings has an exquisite flavor. The person who refuses to be contaminated by worldly opinion is also exquisitely charming.

350、觀物須有自得　勿徒留連光景

　　栽花種竹，玩鶴觀魚，亦要有段自得處。若徒留連光景，玩弄物華，亦吾儒之口耳，釋氏之頑空而已，有何佳趣。

Learn from recreational activities. Don't just kill time.

Growing plants and observing animals are pleasant leisure time activities. If a person knows only to enjoy himself but fails to learn something significant from these activities, he gets only what the Confucian calls "useless shallow knowledge" and what the Buddhist says "meaningless foolish emptiness." What charm does futile pleasure possess?

351、陷於不義　生不若死

山林之士清苦，而逸趣自饒；農野之人鄙略，而天真渾具。若一失身市井馹儈，不若轉死溝壑，神骨猶清。

If forced into doing something dishonest, it is better to die than to live.

An enlightened person without any prominent government position is poor in material comforts but rich with abundant leisure time to enjoy life. Country folks are rustic and crude but are true and honest. It is better to die in poverty to preserve honor than to live a dishonest life for great material comforts.

352、非分之收穫　陷溺之根源

非分之福，無故之穫，非造物之釣餌，即人世之機阱。此處著眼不高，鮮不墮彼術中矣。

Undeserved gains are roots for disastrous downfall.

Undeserved luck and unreasonable gains are either the Creator's snares or traps set by humans to catch prey. Those who fail to insist upon what is morally right have little chance to escape.

353、把握要點　卷舒自在

人生原是傀儡，只要根蒂在手，一線不亂，卷舒自由，行止在我，一毫不受他人提掇，便超出場中矣。

To grasp the control bar is to grasp the freedom.

Life is but a puppet show. He who has the ability to handle life's control bar and to conduct threads smoothly and freely without being controlled or manipulated by other people is beyond this show.

354、利害乃世之常　不若無事為福

一事起則一害生，故天下常以無事為福。讀前人詩云：勸君莫話封侯事，一將功成萬骨枯。又云：天下嘗能萬事平，匣中不惜千年死。雖有雄心猛氣，不覺化為冰霰矣。

Gains and losses are common in life. Nothing is better than peace.

All conflicts cause pain and harm. That is why peace is considered the best thing in the world. A poet in the history once wrote, "Please don't strive for kingship. One general's success is at the price of millions of dead soldiers ." Again he wrote, "If there is peace in the world, there will be no regret for me to leave the precious sword deserted in the case." After having read these words, a person's thirsty for war cannot but be quenched.

355、茫茫世間　矛盾之窟

淫奔之婦，矯而為尼；熱中之人，激而入道。清淨之門，常為淫邪之淵藪也如此。

The vast world is but a den of contradictions.

The wanton woman puts on a nun's habit. An eager pursuer of power and wealth studies Tao. What is clean and holy often becomes the disguise of the immoral and the wicked. What a shame it is!

356、身在局中　心在局外

波浪兼天，舟中不知懼，而舟外者寒心；倡狂罵坐，席上不知警，而席外者咋舌。故君子身雖在事中，心要超事外也。

Although deeply involved, keep a clear head to be objective.

The sky-reaching waves always frighten the people on shore but not necessary frighten those on board. An insolent person yelling abusive words at the feast always scares the bystanders but not necessary its guests. An enlightened person should always keep a clear head to be objective even though he is deeply involved in the event.

357、減繁增靜　安樂之基

人生減省一分，便超脫了一分。如交遊減，便免紛擾；言語減，便寡愆尤；思慮減，則精神不耗；聰明減，則混沌可完。彼不求日減而求日增者，真桎梏此生哉。

The foundation for everlasting peace and happiness is simplifying what is complicated and reinforcing what is peaceful

What is reduced in mundane involvement is what is saved for a happier life. To reduce social activities is to reduce troubles, to reduce words is to reduce regrets, to reduce deliberation is to reduce mental fatigue, and to reduce cleverness is to reduce sharp confrontations. Increasing instead of decreasing mundane involvement puts people in bondage and suffering.

358、滿腔和氣　隨地春風

天運之寒暑易避，人世之炎涼難除；人世之炎涼易除，吾心之冰炭難去。去得此中之冰炭，則滿腔皆和氣，隨地有春風矣。

Be friendly and warm-hearted. The pleasant spring breeze is in all places.

Compared with human's cold shoulders and hot flattery, winter's bitter cold and summer's scorching heat are nothing. Compared with the deep-seated ice in heart, cold shoulders and hot flattery become trifles. After a person has dissolved the ice in his heart, he becomes warm and friendly and finds the pleasant spring breeze wherever he goes.

359、超越口耳之嗜欲　得見人生之真趣

茶不求精而壺亦不燥，酒不求冽而樽亦不空，素琴無絃而常調，短笛無腔而自適。縱難超越羲皇，亦可匹儔嵇阮。

Go beyond sensual pleasures to taste the true joy of life.

As long as there is tea in the teapot, it is not important whether the tea is excellent. So long as there is wine in the wine jar, it does not matter if the wine is of good quality. Play the stringed instrument whenever there is a chance although it is out of tune. Play the flute for self-amusement although the notes are not exactly right. Anyone who holds this kind of attitude towards life can be compared with the seven great followers of Laozi and Zhuangzi - the two great Chinese philosophers - even though not surpasses the great King Fu-xi - the legendary Chinese ruler in ancient China.

360、萬事皆緣　隨遇而安

釋氏隨緣，吾儒素位，四字是渡海的浮囊。蓋世路茫茫，一念求全，則萬緒紛起，隨遇而安，則無入不得矣。

Submit to life's unpredictable course. Feel contented with whatever Providence provides.

Buddha teaches people to submit to life's unpredictable course, and Confucius advises people to be contented with present situation. Both are buoys to help people go across life's vast ocean safely. Life's course is misty. Demanding perfection generates endless troubles. Submitting to life's unpredictable course and feeling contented with whatever Providence provides help people find everlasting peace and happiness.

釀文學199　PG1518

 再譯菜根譚——英漢對照
Vegetable Roots With English Translation

譯　　著	金莉華（Chin Lee-hua）
責任編輯	盧羿珊
圖文排版	周妤靜
封面設計	蔡瑋筠

出版策劃	釀出版
製作發行	秀威資訊科技股份有限公司
	114 台北市內湖區瑞光路76巷65號1樓
	電話：+886-2-2796-3638　傳真：+886-2-2796-1377
	服務信箱：service@showwe.com.tw
	http://www.showwe.com.tw
郵政劃撥	19563868　戶名：秀威資訊科技股份有限公司
展售門市	國家書店【松江門市】
	104 台北市中山區松江路209號1樓
	電話：+886-2-2518-0207　傳真：+886-2-2518-0778
網路訂購	秀威網路書店：http://www.bodbooks.com.tw
	國家網路書店：http://www.govbooks.com.tw
法律顧問	毛國樑　律師
總 經 銷	聯合發行股份有限公司
	231新北市新店區寶橋路235巷6弄6號4F
	電話：+886-2-2917-8022　傳真：+886-2-2915-6275

出版日期	2016年8月　BOD一版
定　　價	300元

國家圖書館出版品預行編目

再譯菜根譚：英漢對照 / 金莉華譯著. -- 一版. -- 臺北市：
釀出版, 2016.08
　　面；　公分. -- (釀文學；199)
BOD版
中英對照
ISBN 978-986-445-118-0(平裝)

1. 修身

192.1　　　　　　　　　　　　　　　　105008454

讀者回函卡

感謝您購買本書，為提升服務品質，請填妥以下資料，將讀者回函卡直接寄回或傳真本公司，收到您的寶貴意見後，我們會收藏記錄及檢討，謝謝！
如您需要了解本公司最新出版書目、購書優惠或企劃活動，歡迎您上網查詢或下載相關資料：http:// www.showwe.com.tw

您購買的書名：_____

出生日期：_____年_____月_____日

學歷：□高中 (含) 以下　　□大專　　□研究所 (含) 以上

職業：□製造業　□金融業　□資訊業　□軍警　□傳播業　□自由業
　　　□服務業　□公務員　□教職　　□學生　□家管　　□其它_____

購書地點：□網路書店　□實體書店　□書展　□郵購　□贈閱　□其他

您從何得知本書的消息？

　□網路書店　□實體書店　□網路搜尋　□電子報　□書訊　□雜誌
　□傳播媒體　□親友推薦　□網站推薦　□部落格　□其他_____

您對本書的評價：(請填代號　1.非常滿意　2.滿意　3.尚可　4.再改進)

　封面設計____　版面編排____　內容____　文／譯筆____　價格____

讀完書後您覺得：

　□很有收穫　□有收穫　□收穫不多　□沒收穫

對我們的建議：_____

_____

_____

_____

11466
台北市內湖區瑞光路 76 巷 65 號 1 樓

秀威資訊科技股份有限公司　　　收

BOD 數位出版事業部

....

（請沿線對折寄回，謝謝！）

姓　　名：_____　年齡：_____　性別：□女　□男

郵遞區號：□□□□□

地　　址：_____

聯絡電話：(日) _____　(夜) _____

E-mail：_____